MORE LOST
THAN FOUND

MORE LOST THAN FOUND

FINDING A WAY BACK TO FAITH

by Jared Herd

THOMAS NELSON
Since 1798

NASHVILLE   DALLAS   MEXICO CITY   RIO DE JANEIRO

Published in Nashville, Tennessee, by Thomas Nelson. Thomas Nelson is a registered trademark of Thomas Nelson, Inc.

Thomas Nelson, Inc., titles may be purchased in bulk for educational, business, fund-raising, or sales promotional use. For information, please e-mail SpecialMarkets@ThomasNelson.com.

Unless otherwise noted, Scripture quotations are taken from the HOLY BIBLE: NEW INTERNATIONAL VERSION®. © 1973, 1978, 1984 by International Bible Society. Used by permission of Zondervan Publishing House. All rights reserved.

Library of Congress Cataloging-in-Publication Data

Herd, Jared, 1981–
    More lost than found : finding a way back to faith / Jared Herd.
      p. cm.
    Includes bibliographical references and index.
    ISBN 978-1-4002-0303-1
    1. Christian life. 2. Christianity—United States—21st century. I. Title. II. Title: Finding a way back to faith.
    BV4501.3.H465 2011
    248.4—dc22   2011000206

Printed in the United States of America

11 12 13 14 15 QG 5 4 3 2 1

This book is dedicated to my wife, Rosanna. Without you, I'm afraid I'd still think the words I write are more important than the life I live. Thank you for showing me what it means to be fully engaged with the gift of life. You are on every page of this book. You are my best friend. I love you.

CONTENTS

CONTENTS

PROLOGUE

I vaguely remember finding Jesus when I was a child, but I vividly recall losing him. A few months shy of my seventh birthday I walked down the aisle of my southern-fried Baptist church, greeted by my pastor, parents, and a handful of deacons in JCPenney suits. My father was a minister in that church, and a few weeks after I walked down the aisle, he baptized me during a half-empty Sunday night service. I loved my father in the way someone six years into his life should. He was rugged like the Marlboro man but tender as a mollusk inside, and he spoke of Jesus as if he'd actually met him. When I arose from the water, my skin was cold like hell is hot, but my soul was clean as a river-smoothed stone. My father asserted with bravado to the mostly vacant room that his younger boy's name was now written in the Lamb's Book of Life, as if he had written it himself.

Seven years later, my family's carefully pruned image was shattered when my father's affair became public. My faith in God was built by his words, words left hollow by his scandal. During a Sunday night prayer service, my mother, brother, and I stood to ask for prayer in front of a sparse but committed crowd, and there I stood like a wounded war pony just a few feet from that same baptistery. That night I was surrounded by some of those same deacons in those same JCPenney suits, with my mother's face as red as the Georgia clay the church was built on.

I didn't know what sins my father had committed, but I knew this church had robbed him of his ability to be happy or to be home long before the choir started whispering about his transgressions. I watched him die there in that church while he gave his life to others. As what was left of my family stood there, I wanted to run away from this religious circus. My faith died in the place where it began, and alas, I was more lost than found.

Several years later I returned to the Christian faith, but not like a soldier returns home, more like the Red Cross goes to a storm ravaged city. I didn't return with deeper commitments to old beliefs; I came searching for a new way to relate to Jesus.

I grew up believing Christianity was about what we believe

while we are on Earth and about where we go when we die. End of story. While I am not negating either of those, the assumptions I've had about the Christian faith for most of my life tend to remove my faith from my everyday life. Growing up, Christianity always felt like something "other," a random group of people who went about their everyday lives, gathered around their cosmic assumptions to do life together, and shared their opinions about how to live until you die.

I would go to church, and then I would reenter life, which was with people who didn't share those assumptions. This always felt like an unnatural divide, and my life developed a "fishbowl effect." The fishbowl effect was a guilt, a twinge, an inability to relate to the life I actually lived. Perhaps you have felt that effect too.

Perhaps you've always wondered how music, movies, friends, or anything on the outside of a sanitized Christianity could relate to your life inside of it. Perhaps because of the disconnect and the friction it causes, you abandoned the fishbowl a long time ago. If you are anything like me, you thought that when you left the fishbowl you were leaving the Christian faith behind. I am convinced the fishbowl is what made us feel lost, not the Scriptures. Understanding that there is a big difference between those two is a critical building block in putting our faith back together.

In these pages, I'm inviting you on a path that moves away from a faith that is just about agreeing with a set of beliefs. That first path, the one that tries to put a tidy bow around life, can suppress our human frailty because it rushes to answer questions and fill in blanks. In fact, there's almost a panic that comes, right? The tidy path can offer us some certainty and a degree of comfort, but it cuts short a genuine spiritual journey before it ever begins.

Have you ever talked to a Christian who gave a scripted answer to a tough question? If they had answered your question with less certainty and more honesty, would you have believed them more? The way Christian faith is most often expressed in our culture doesn't offer us tools for the spiritual journey. Instead, it's much better at giving us scripted answers so we can opt out of our spiritual curiosity. But I don't mean to lay all the blame at the church's stoop.

I think it is less about the church and its failure to equip us than it is about the drive inside of every human not to leave any stone unturned, any question unanswered. But there's an equal drive to have every question answered, and that's the origin of tidy Christianity. If you think about it for a moment though, that path can be devoid of trust—trust in God, in others, and in completion of Christ's work on the cross. Salvation did not come merely so we could sign a petition of beliefs. It came so we could have a genuine, intimate relationship with God. We need to recover the vulnerability of the spiritual journey even when it goes against our very nature for certainty—because that is a reflection of real relationship.

The conversation in this book has implications for culture as a whole, not just for those of us who have been to church. We are living in interesting days in America. Every time we turn on the television, we are reminded that the political, economic, and social climate of our world is changing. In this state of flux, perhaps it is easy to forget that the spiritual climate is changing as well. While we live in a nation that has been deeply influenced and governed with a Christian worldview, we are a generation of young men and women who, for the most part, are rejecting that worldview and that story.

At the same time, we find ourselves in a culture that has many prime-time television shows, hit songs, *New York Times* best sellers, and Oscar-winning films with deeply spiritual messages. If we look closely enough, culture is telling us that spirituality is en vogue. Culture itself has become the church. As Christopher Partridge noted in his book by the same title, there has been a "re-enchantment of the West."[1] But why is Jesus rarely the first person people go to when seeking answers to life's biggest questions? We are in a unique cultural situation where John Mayer might shape our spiritual journey as much as the Scriptures.

A genuine faith, one that is "in the world but not of the world" is comfortable engaging with culture, evaluating secular spirituality from the firm ground of Christian spirituality. What our entertainment media seems to recognize is that life itself is a spiritual journey, and we will be better off if we remove some religious labels. After all, we generally use labels to identify someone or something we don't understand; we rarely use them to identify ourselves. What if we started with the premise that we all got dropped here into this place called Earth, and we are all looking for a story to live in, a context for our lives? That drive to find answers and truth is emerging everywhere; except most of the time, Jesus is not the destination people are driving toward.

Oftentimes, the particular label we choose frees us from having to take the journey, but if we are honest, we are all in the same predicament. I believe there is a false gap for those who seek encounters with the divine and believe the church is *not* the place for divine encounters. We are a profoundly spiritual generation, and I believe Christianity is a spiritual endeavor, not just a cold belief system or worldview disassociated from meaningful daily life. Hopefully, this conversation will reengage you to see how Christianity not only comes with insight and meaning for daily life but also enhances those "other" parts the church has ignored.

• • •

I am fascinated with the life and ministry of Jesus. The beloved Jesus that the Gospels reveal to us is not a Savior untouched by the needs and mess of his own day, quartering himself off in the holiest of holies. We don't even find him as distant as Moses, coming down from the mountain through billows of smoke to reveal the sacred words from above. In contrast, we find the people's Savior. A Savior with as much grit and pluck as his audience. We can't ever separate Jesus from the cultural backdrop he chose to enter. He doesn't theologize disconnected from the culture of his day or deliver an application apart from the felt needs of his audience. Shockingly, the message of Jesus is for the people. They didn't have to dust the cobwebs off his words or reach for a commentary as we often do.

In the present day, the message of Christianity is shaped in church buildings before it goes to the streets. Perhaps the violent rejection of that message by those on the outside isn't an issue with Jesus—it's an issue with how the Savior has been translated for them. The kingdom of God would be better served if we conducted the same kind of "marketplace" theology that Jesus did. A theology that shows a reverence for the culture based on love, a theology that chooses to enter its contemporary context instead of shake its finger at it.

During the past ten years, I have traveled the country, lived on both sides of it, and met with thousands of high school and college students. The conversations I've had were in churches, classrooms, schools, coffee shops, waffle shops, and one water park. They took place in urban cores and one-horse towns, in cars, on buses, and sometimes on horses. During those conversations, many labeled themselves "Christian" while many did not. Many of those Christians have gone to church faithfully and still felt more lost than found.

The Christians and nonbelievers, however, had one thing in common—they are wrestling fiercely with their place in the spiritual journey. This book has been inspired by those conversations, and it's for anyone who is wrestling or looking for language and a foothold to engage with God in a genuine way, a way that is not divorced from everyday life. There are millions of us, inquisitive and articulate young men and women, feeling disillusioned with Christianity yet looking for a place to wrestle with our questions. This book, as much as it was just for me when I started writing years ago, is for all of you now. It's for us.

ONE

TYLENOL AND DUCT TAPE

LOST IN TRANSLATION

Welcome to planet Earth. It is located 93 million miles from this ball of energy we call the sun. It is one of nine planets. At least that was the count when I was in fourth grade. Apparently it is getting warmer.

The other day I was in an airport, and as I was coming off the escalator, there was a limousine driver holding a sign with "Mr. Jones" written on it. I thought about how nice that would be as I trudged through the terminal on my way to rent a car. After a ridiculously long wait in line and the attendant's incredible amount of tapping on the Hertz keyboard, I made my way to the cheapest rental they had—a foreign car with a three-stroke engine, a glorified lawn mower. If this car was short on amenities, it had less by way of reliability. Somehow, it blew a tire as I was driving it through Atlanta at one o'clock in the morning.

I found myself stranded in an unfamiliar part of town,

so I was quite nervous as I waited for a tow truck. As I stood there debating whether to hide in my trunk, I thought about how nice it would have been to tell the limo driver I was Mr. Jones. He wouldn't have known. He surely hadn't met the guy before. I wondered all of this, of course, because I am sure Mr. Jones had a much different welcome to Atlanta than I did. He was probably asleep in a Hilton while I wandered a freeway looking for fragments of a tire.

Perhaps there was a time when people came into the world and a limo was waiting. They had parents who loved them and each other, a place that felt like home, and eventually a sense that they mattered and belonged. Most of us didn't arrive here that way. Maybe babies are smarter than we think. Maybe they cry because they realize they are now here and this life isn't going to be a limo ride on the way to the Hilton. More often than not, it is going to feel more like a Thunderdome journey on a six-lane freeway in a sardine-can sedan.

Preschool was the first traumatic experience of my life I can distinctly remember. My mom and I had a daily ritual. She would pull up at the preschool to drop me off, and I would cry as soon as I saw the building. When the door opened to exit the car, instead of getting out of it, I climbed into the backseat and kicked anyone who tried to make me leave the car. Every day like clockwork. School led to tears, and tears led to kicking.

We make some assumptions about how life works and what we are going to have to do to make it through. One of my earliest assumptions was that home was safe and any-place that didn't involve my mom wasn't. As we grow up, we make more assumptions about life. Some of them are right—many of them are probably wrong—but they impact our way of viewing the world that we live in and how we think about it. As we get older, we keep doing this. The incoming fresh-man has a panic attack the first day of ninth grade based on assumptions. The sixteen-year-old studies hours on end with the assumption that he can control his own future. There are things we are all afraid of, mostly based on assumptions. Dating. Tests. The future. Those fears aren't by chance. They all come from assumptions.

An Incomplete History of Rap Music

As you read this, there is a tribe somewhere in a foreign land wearing tribal gear, performing a tribal ritual to appeal to tribal gods. They have no computers or cell phones. I feel it's important to tell you that I do not write that as a scholar, a world traveler, or an imperialist, but rather as someone who has seen a few episodes on the Discovery Channel. That tribe knows nothing about your life, and you likely know nothing about theirs. While all of us have our own culture, ultimately where and when we live determines how we see and look at the world. (For example, my view of life while living in America in the twenty-first century is much different from what someone would have thought about life living in Omaha in 1909—or in London in 1509. We would probably have different opinions on everything.)

It would be fascinating to get an inside look at that tribal culture. Why do they sing the songs they do? Why do they dress the way they do? Has anyone in that culture ever questioned the way things are? If they wore a pair of blue jeans would they find them to be more comfortable than loincloths? Would this spark a denim revolution and upset the tribal gods?

Chances are, no one there has ever thought about it. It's just the way things are. In the same way, we don't really think about our culture that we live in as being that fascinating; it's just the way things are. But what if we could step back and ask some questions about it?

- Why do we do what we do?
- How does what we do impact what we think?
- What does what we do say about how we think about spiritual things?

Are we confined by the same kind of old world trepidation as the distant tribe? People who follow Jesus (or any faith for that matter) in our culture are traditionally nervous when it comes to their broader culture. In our time and place, from the movies to the music to the Internet to high school campuses, if it stinks of anything contrary to our beliefs, if it has a negative label, then we should leave it alone. I even heard a preacher say that Christians are in a culture war and we need to fight in it. The preacher's assumption is that anything outside the Christian culture has nothing to add to spiritual truth. In fact, it's a cancer to the truth.

The broader culture isn't just a wasteland of sin and debasement, and if we listen closely, we may hear it telling us something. If we are all "dropped here" and make assumptions about this world, then culture is our world's way of sharing those assumptions. Culture reflects the way things are. So everything that is happening in our culture is telling us something about what is going on. Rap music, for instance, tells us something about the world we live in. Rap music is fundamentally about power. And who is it that listens? Primarily those who don't have power.

It is hard to conceive of a powerful judge or senator rattling my windows at a stoplight. So with a song and a stereo we can feel a sense of control; we embrace the illusion that we have something we really don't possess. This is why the primary market for rap music isn't successful businesspeople. And yet, rap is a hugely popular genre, especially among young people. Why would a suburban, fairly wealthy, upper-class young man or woman want to try to identify with music about violence, sexual deviation, and growing up poor? Why did this music not even exist thirty years ago?

The church might say that rap music is a problem. But is the problem really that so many people seem to identify with it? Wouldn't a distant culture look at our contemporary moment and see this as odd too? What if a teenage guy who is blaring his rap music went to church at some point and realized that he identified more with the words of a rap song than he did with the words of a pastor? Did the pastor rail against of the content of the music and never ask questions about why it is so popular and has far more influence than he does?

Somewhere in the recent past, young men and women in our culture began to make some observations about our world, and they decided that things were unfair. Rap music is about more than musical taste—it is an anthem declaring to the rest of the world how a generation feels. Rap music, whether the pastor likes it or not, isn't just selling records. It is reflecting a worldview.[1]

An Incomplete History of Adolescence

If there had been rap music in Omaha in 1909, I don't think it would have had much of an audience. So why do so many now seem so angry? People have obviously always gotten angry. Any basic reading of the Bible tells us that. But when you look at our culture from the outside, say, if those people in Omaha then saw us now, what is normal to us would be evidence to them that something is wrong. If culture reflects the way things are, then couldn't we look at American culture, say, fifty years ago, and draw some assumptions about the way things were then? Fifty years ago, a mom and her daughter would probably dress in similar clothes. They would probably listen to very similar music. They would watch the same movies. They would, for the most part, have the same vocabulary.

You have probably noticed that now there are huge differences between your interests and your parents' interests. You don't listen to the same music. You don't wear the same clothes. Mom's jeans and a fanny pack aren't going to score many invitations to dinner. You don't even use a lot of the same words. Your parents might need a translator to understand a conversation between you and your friends. You may share a house, but you don't share much else. We don't ask a lot of questions about this. But the way things are isn't indicative of the way things were. Your America and mine is much different from our parents' America.

Perhaps we can chalk it up to the fact that things are always changing. But what if our parents turned their clocks back fifty years from their childhood? Interestingly, things weren't that much different between their parents and them. Your great-grandparents had a lot in common with your grandparents when they were in high school. The further back you go in this time line, the smaller the gap of similar experience gets.

For thousands of years, there wasn't much separation between teenage culture and everyone else in society. Actually, there wasn't really a "teenage culture" at all. People basically went from childhood to adulthood, and this thing we call "adolescence" didn't even exist. But then life spans started getting longer, and the differences between kids and parents started widening. Eventually the kids couldn't relate to the parents anymore, and youth culture was born. It is tempting to blame technology, that its rapid advances created separation, but was that really the cause? When cavemen invented the wheel, did this lead to a cave-teen rebellion? Something tells me this isn't about cell phones, Google, and iTunes. Something about the fabric of life is different.

Thousands of years ago, hundreds of years ago even, the goal of parents and grandparents was to pass along their culture to the children. Every culture had its story and worldview—who they were, why they mattered, and what the purpose of life was. The goal between generations was to transmit and preserve these values. They knew something that we probably believe but don't really experience: understanding the way things were helps us create the way things are.

Children born hundreds of years ago were born into a story, and parents made sure their children knew that story and felt a part of it. So, going to visit your grandparents was an important experience because it taught you not just who they were, it taught you about who *you* were too. In the late eighteenth century and early nineteenth century, all of this began to change. Culture no longer centered on getting passed down; it became about advancement in all forms— looking forward instead of looking back.

In the history books, the Industrial Revolution acts as the big marker in our cultural time line. By around 1850, Britain, America, and other industrialized countries were in full swing making locomotives, sewing machines, tanks, and funny hats. The focus shifted from transmitting culture to building railroads, textiles, steamboats, and more funny hats. To fuel the production, the population in cities exploded so that people could be close to the machines that made more machines.

Before then, there was no need to live so close to other people. On the surface, it all seemed great. Everything got faster while everyone got richer. In the meantime, because people were desperate to build and grow and make more, children were no longer at peace on the farm with the family, learning about the way things were so they could understand who they were. Instead, they went to work. They were building a new way of life in these strange centers of civilization called *cities*.

Interestingly, even at this point in our cultural time line, the word *adolescent* didn't exist. There was still the age-old transition from childhood to adulthood. Even in the nineteenth century, by age sixteen or seventeen, you had adult responsibilities and didn't spend your nights journaling in rage because somebody made fun of you at school and you didn't have a date to the prom. But soon after, seemingly all of a sudden, the sixteen- and seventeen-year-olds started to change. They didn't seem to make the transition to adulthood as smoothly as their predecessors.

Even more interesting, G. Stanley Hall, a psychologist, wrote a book in 1904 titled *Adolescence*.[2] Hall noticed this problem and said there seems to be a third stage to life, between childhood and adulthood. Thus, teenage culture as we know it was born. The first rap song hadn't been written, but the seeds of change were there.

This was about a two-year process; then adolescents would become adults. But as time went on, there was no slowing down the progress of civilization, and there was no slowing down the damage that was being done to children either. There was no longer a story to be a part of. For children, the world became just a place to survive and feed the machine. The frustration of adolescence was the result. As America grew, the role of adolescence grew too. America suddenly had a lot of young men and women who didn't really know what to do with themselves.

By the 1960s, America couldn't go back on itself. Adolescence was a new constant in our culture. From one perspective, things were pretty good—prosperity and progress were the ultimate values, and there was plenty to go around. But people between ages thirteen and twenty-one didn't seem to like it. They started singing songs and holding rallies all in the name of frustration. They forged their own society, which was "anti" society. They were the children of industry and advancement, and they all shared the same sentiment—it didn't work for them. At the same time, divorces became more frequent. Family life was no longer nuclear with a mother, father, and siblings. "Family" became anyone your age who felt like you did. How did building some railroads lead to all of this?

When people don't feel like they belong anywhere, they find somewhere to belong. Adolescence became about finding somewhere to belong. Until youth felt like they belonged or mattered, they just stayed in adolescence, a transitory state of figuring things out.

A Brave New World?

If you fast-forward to today, adolescence is longer than it has ever been. People graduate from college and don't really know where they belong. Our parents still pay our cell phone bills while we struggle to make sense of it all. Humankind has always struggled with purpose, but never has there been a time such as this in which the world leaves an entire demographic on its own to make sense of it all.

Our world still revolves around progress. More than ever. And as long as it does, this problem isn't going away. Think about your own family. You probably feel a deeper sense of connectedness to your friends than your parents. You probably feel like your parents help provide certain things for you, but they aren't helping you figure out where you belong here and what really matters. The reason you are closer to your friends is that they give you a sense that you do matter and you do belong. This is true for young men and women across the board, whether they come from Christian homes, divorced homes, or atheist homes.

The gallery of people from Omaha in 1909 might think we're odd. But we don't. We just assume this is the way it is, but it shouldn't be this way.

So where does that leave culture, and where does that leave us? If you are anything like me, a steady stream of various voices is shaping your worldview. We stand on a quote from our favorite movie or a quote from Scripture, sometimes not even knowing the difference. We inform ourselves with film, music, books, art, and whatever else may grab us. We'll even have a pinch of Buddhism if we are daring.[3] Whatever the sources may be that shape us, one thing is becoming increasingly certain for this generation: the voice of Jesus is getting drowned out. It isn't that he has competition either. It's just that his voice has come through a body of people, perhaps a church, that didn't translate it in a way that stuck. It's not their fault. And it's not ours. It's just the way things are . . . but only if you let them stay that way.

• • •

I love the church. As far back as I can remember, I was sitting in a church somewhere on a Sunday. But now when I read the Scriptures and about this compelling figure named Jesus, I can't imagine him being here and not connecting with those who are sitting on the outside and don't even care to look in. First-century Palestine was a place of poverty and suffering. It was a place where taxes were about 90 percent of an individual's income and the money went to glorify Rome and build more palaces for the Caesars. Jesus had something to say about that.

The life and ministry of Jesus have affected the world like nothing else the world has ever known, but a surface reading of the Scripture leads us to believe he was trying to change his culture, not necessarily cultures for thousands of years to come. He was rallying for change, turning the system on its head, which led to his death. If Jesus was concerned with the context then, wouldn't he be concerned with it now? Wouldn't he make himself relevant to those who feel like life isn't fair? I bet he'd have a lot to say to those of us in pain.

The message of Jesus is timeless and beautiful. For thousands of years, the church has been a champion of that message. In my opinion, that makes her timeless and beautiful too. But churches and culture have always been tied together. It is impossible to think about any form of faith apart from the culture it finds itself in. There have been many times in human history when following Jesus began to look different because of changes in culture. In fact, the way we follow Jesus now is much different than the way people in the first century would have followed him. Some may think it is blasphemous or heretical to allow the culture to help shape a timeless message. I would argue that this is already happening and that all of us understand and relate to Jesus through the lens of our experiences and our culture. It is a paradox, but to stay the same, the gospel must always be changing.[4]

Somehow, amid the disconnect of the newfangled phase called adolescence, the culture of our parents and their parents shaped the way we understand what it means to follow Jesus. But it was probably distant and disconnected from our everyday experiences. Perhaps in this unique culture of abandonment and jadedness, we can find a message that is timely and timeless.

I was in Seattle recently, and I noticed they had lots and lots of bodies of water. I am from Georgia originally, and I know three words for bodies of water: *lake, river,* or *ocean.* So, as I was being driven to my hotel, I would see water, and I would make a comment about what a cool lake I saw. This was until I was corrected and told it wasn't a lake, it was a *sound.* A what? I would see another and say that is a cool river, until I was corrected again. Wrong, that is a *fjord.* A what? Everyone there seemed to know these words. I did not.

I heard a pastor talk about a similar experience, and he said the more a culture has of something, the more words it has to describe it. There are very few words for white stuff that falls from the sky in Los Angeles. *Snow* is the only one that comes to mind. Yet if you go to places in Canada, there are more words for snow. The same pastor went on to say we live in a world where words like *bipolar, depression, anxiety, rehabilitation, ADD, ADHD, manic depression, schizophrenia, suicide*—the list goes on and on—are common. We all know what they mean. In our parents' generation, most of these words weren't around.[5] You were either crazy or normal. There wasn't much that Tylenol and duct tape couldn't fix.

Abandonment, a feeling so central to the time between childhood and adulthood, has changed the cultural landscape. Our vocabulary tells us so. The message of Jesus we have received doesn't fit as well anymore. Does he even know what any of this psychobabble is? We doubt it, and we conclude he can't identify with us and we can't identify with him. We identify with music, film, and friends, all the while suppressing that hunch that we're ticking him off and driving him crazy. So is the problem Jesus? Or is the problem how we have been told to think about him? A bunch of stuff we couldn't control—the world we were born into and the churches our parents took us to—had unmitigated influence about how we think of Jesus and on the shape of our spiritual journey. Maybe it isn't that Jesus doesn't fit. Maybe it is just hard to convince us we are sinners when we feel like we have been sinned against our whole lives.

When I read about Jesus, he seems to find ways to make himself fit. And maybe he looks at the messages being tossed around about him and wants them to change. We are hurting. Things don't make sense. We are bleeding, and all we have are Tylenol and duct tape.

TWO

SHATTERING THE FISHBOWL

THE SACRED SECULAR

E very generation has a defining moment, a moment when everyone collectively faces adversity, evil, or sweeping change. No one is left out, regardless of ethnic or economic status. I love to hear my grandparents talk about World War II, their generation's defining moment. Some guy across the ocean wanted to take over the world, and he was doing a pretty good job of making that vision a reality. America tried to avoid it, but eventually some people who liked this guy brought the war over here, so we went over there and settled it. It is a great story. Good-versus-evil stuff. The powerful crushed the weak, only to be overtaken by something more powerful than them. My grandfathers fought in it. Yours probably did too.

If that was their defining moment, then September 11, 2001, was ours.

All of us awoke one morning in our normal routines

only to turn on televisions and realize that things were far from normal. Unlike World War II, this seemed to come from nowhere. Who were we fighting? Why were they fighting us? In the coming months, words like *war on terror* and *Taliban* were inserted into our daily vocabulary. Before that, I would have guessed Taliban was a cough medicine. One good thing about September 11 is that everyone began to examine the way things were and if they should be that way. Everyone seemed to have different answers too. One thing that everyone seemed to agree on was that we needed a higher power in our time of need. Every place of worship in America was flooded with people who hadn't gone in years and by those who had never gone. Because there was something obviously, undeniably wrong, everyone was searching for answers.

Before September 11, one assumption people had was that America was moving further and further away from being a spiritual nation. Progress, money, and status were our gods. After September 11, there seemed to be a return to the spiritual. Not just in church, but in culture as a whole. Many of the songs carried a spiritual message with them. Hollywood, which was blamed for a rise in violence, sexuality, and moral decay, began to make movies by the bundle that went beyond entertainment to have a spiritual message too. Movies like *Walk to Remember* and *Passion of the Christ* were huge successes, and Hollywood executives scrambled to make more of them. Television got in on the game too. Three major networks debuted shows dealing with UFOs. People everywhere began to ask questions and make assumptions about what they couldn't see in ways that haven't happened in a long time.

But that return to spirituality in America wasn't a return to Christianity.[1] Spirituality itself is our new religion. Jesus doesn't seem to have a spot at the table in the spiritual conversation. Isn't America supposed to be Christian? Wasn't it founded by Christians who came over here from England? Didn't fifty-two of the fifty-five men who signed the Declaration of Independence believe that being an American was synonymous with being a Christian?

When I was in high school, Marilyn Manson made a huge splash in our culture and drew an opinion from everyone. He was a rock star who went way outside the bounds of normal to get attention, and he gained a huge following with his message. You don't hear much about him anymore. He is largely irrelevant. The other day, I saw him on television. He was dating a Hollywood actress who has a huge following, and they had released a sex tape. The only way the irrelevant Manson became relevant again was by dating someone who is. He was on TV now not because of who he is but because of her. I don't know if it is safe to relate Jesus to Marilyn Manson, but Jesus' place in the spiritual conversation seems similar.

In our culture, for many he is a distant memory without much relevance, except when he affects something or someone who does have relevance. People rail against him as the reason our president led us into war. People assume he is the catalyst for anti-abortion or anti-homosexual rights. No one really listens to him outside the walls of church. People make assumptions about him based on how he seems to impact what matters to them. Not only Jesus, but also the words that go with him only matter to a select few.

A hundred years ago in America, a word like *sin* would have made sense to everyone, in or out of church. Today sin doesn't have much punch to it. It has been emptied of its meaning in our culture. I was reminded of this when I saw a television commercial for a chocolate company describing their product as "sinfully delicious." A hundred years ago, this kind of association was unthinkable. A product wouldn't have been marketed as sinful. The word *sin* has more marketing panache than spiritual truth. On the flip side, a word like *karma* would have had no real meaning a hundred years ago in America. *Karma* is rooted in Eastern religions to describe how past and present actions affect our future. In America currently, *karma* is far better understood than a word like *sin*. How did things change? And where did Jesus go?

The Country Club

It is not that Jesus has fallen off the map—culture has relocated him to a distant corner of it. The other day I was flipping through the channels, and I noticed that there were three Christian networks on the air. If you turn on the radio, there are a few of the same kind of stations—playing all Christian, all the time. There are bookstores where you can buy Christian books, pictures, even "testamints," which apparently make your breath smell holy. (Wow. Is Listerine the name of a pagan god?)

Most towns in America have Christian schools, and there is usually a Christian college nearby. Someone even showed me an iCross, a device that you can place on top of your iPod to make it the shape of the cross. There are Christian movies. There is Christian *everything*. It is possible to be driving with your friends from a Christian school on your way to see a Christian movie while you listen to Christian radio and chew on Christian mints. That car probably has a fish on the back of it too. In our culture, *Christian* isn't a noun proclaiming the center of someone's identity or spiritual life. It is an adjective convincing us that something has been sanitized and is now safe to use.[2]

When I was a kid, our family lived next to a country club. We weren't members—you had to pay a lot of money to play golf and eat there. My dad didn't play golf, and he wasn't the kind of guy to dine with people who did. I had friends who were members, though. They took lessons there on everything from swimming to etiquette. They ate there, and their parents made sure they spent most of their summers with the other country club kids. I didn't ever have a desire to join. I didn't play golf or feel the need to wear golf-related apparel. I'm not slamming country clubs. I just didn't see a need to join.

In a way, I felt about that country club the same way many of us feel about church. If we are honest, doesn't Christianity sometimes seem like a club or society you have to join, not a person you have to follow? The drift you have in your life taking you away from Christianity isn't because you are losing your capacity for spirituality. Perhaps you just lost your capacity for things that seem exclusive and too sanitized.

Sacred versus Secular

The way we don't ask questions about culture at large is, in my experience, the same for Christians and "Christian culture" (a term I'm not fond of, by the way). We just assume it is how things are.

I used to keep a fishbowl on my desk at home. I have to travel a lot to speak, sometimes for two or three days, and this didn't prove to be good for the health of the fish. I would dump extra fish food in the bowl, hoping the fish would have plenty to eat while I was gone. Every time I returned, the fish were floating at the top. Eventually I quit buying them. I was spacing out one afternoon when I still had a fish,

26

daydreaming between e-mails, and the fish seemed fascinating to me because they stayed in their bowl and seemed so happy. I always wondered if they looked around the room and felt a little cheated. Here I had the entire apartment and they were confined to their little bowl, the outside world always in view but never in reach.

Somewhere along the way, Christians began to treat God as if he lives inside of churches and wants you to consume only the things labeled "Christian," but everywhere else in culture he is nonexistent. It is a complete bifurcation where certain things are *spiritual* and then there is everything else. There is the church we go to or the Christian stuff we participate in, and then there is the rest of our week.

In our culture, God is in a fishbowl, too, and it seems like we're intentionally starving him. We go somewhere to pay homage to something we can't see, and then we return to reality. But there is a better, more connected way. We can either choose to stay in the fishbowl where everything is safe, or we can go out into the world where it is not. For years, people have called this the divide between the sacred and the secular. In America we believe in this divide; we even legislate it. The church and state shall be separate. The Christian worldview we have adopted places God in a fishbowl, while we live in reality. So, to experience something we cannot see, we must go into the fishbowl. Or we must build the fishbowl bigger so we can live in it, go to school in it, bowl in it, and have fresh breath in it.

Neo-Gentiles

Ultimately, the fishbowl, this sign of sanitization and exclusivity, becomes a wall that keeps some in and a lot out. While it insulates and protects us, it is a rigid reminder of who is a goldfish and who is not. It creates clean categories for what we can listen to and watch, who it is we can trust, who goes to heaven, and who goes to hell. But the categories can do a lot of damage too. The early church, shortly after the empty tomb, found itself in a similar struggle.

The Bible is filled with all sorts of interesting exchanges that I didn't know existed when I was a kid. From the perspective of the Bible, there were two groups of people. There were Jewish people, and there was everybody else. This "everybody else" was the Gentiles. Peter, who was with Jesus when he was alive, was Jewish. Paul, who was not with Jesus, was Jewish too. Both of these guys are central figures in the New Testament, yet you find them in opposition in the book of Galatians. In that book, Paul gave a very colorful commentary. The primary issue at hand was: "Since Jesus is risen, is his movement still Jewish, or is it something new entirely?"

If it was Jewish, then the rules the Jewish people lived by still applied. If it was something new entirely, then the Jewish customs need not apply. Jesus didn't stick around to explain it. Peter believed that the Jewish customs still applied. Paul said they didn't. Thus, the first Christian theological debate.

Paul wrote, "When Peter came to Antioch, I opposed him to his face, because he was clearly in the wrong."[3] Peter believed Gentile followers of Jesus should be circumcised, which was a Jewish custom but not a Gentile one. Most of the book of Galatians is spent navigating the issue.

Ultimately Peter was trying to create a country club, and the price of admission was circumcision. Peter was trying to build a wall, and Paul was trying to widen the doors. Paul recognized that Peter was putting the Gentiles into a crisis they didn't need to be in. Paul was essentially saying, "Why are you adding things to the message of Jesus?" I don't think Peter's intentions were evil, but his perspective, in my opinion, was too black-and-white, and it shows the kind of dynamic we're talking about here.

The issue centered on circumcision, but couldn't we also say that circumcision made things certain and simple? Paul was willing to let things be ambiguous and undefined, to let the Good News shape people where they were instead of indoctrinating them in a cultural framework that made no sense. Perhaps we need Paul to remind us of that, two thousand years later. The Christian faith isn't an organization with rules and boundaries, terms and conditions for admittance. The Christian faith is an organism that changes and has the ability to be fluid.

As much as I appreciate Paul, I never liked reading his letters as much as I liked reading the accounts of Jesus. I always thought he had a tendency to add red tape to the red letters. But Paul also tore the walls down so the Gentiles could get in. When I realized that, I began to love Paul. He understood that Jesus transcends our cultural boundaries and shattered the fishbowl that Peter was trying to create.

I can empathize with the Galatians. Many of them started getting circumcised because they thought that was what you were supposed to do to fit in. They loved Jesus, and when pressed, they just hopped into the fishbowl. They were in a crisis they didn't have to be in. Joining the circumcision country club isn't what Jesus intended.

In many ways, the Gentiles' story is our story. And I'm not sure the fishbowl is what God had in mind for us. While some of us hop in and stay, many of us hop out and decide not to return. Many live with the guilt of not being able to do it. But do we need to be in this crisis?

We may not be called Gentiles anymore, but we are a generation that isn't united in skin color, economic status, education, or geographic location. We are united in our abandonment, coming together in our sense of wandering the world, wondering if we can ever assimilate into it.

Abandonment makes us citizens of a unique culture. We have been branded by advertisements, coveted by marketers, and dictated to by churches and schools. And yet we're largely left alone to make sense of it all. I do not know what your relationship to the Christian fishbowl has been. If you were raised in it, perhaps you have lived long enough to appreciate what it has given you. Perhaps you jumped out, and you have no plans of jumping back in. If that is you, to reminisce about your childhood faith experience can lead to pain or indifference, or a combination of both.

Either way, the strain you feel doesn't come from a lack of spirituality. It doesn't come from an indifference to things that really matter. I would guess the opposite is true. You do care about things that do matter. You long for justice where there isn't any. You can be overheard at coffee shops telling friends you care about them. You are deeply spiritual, perhaps more than you have ever been.

You don't need an insulated world—you know the world is a mess. You don't need a sanitized version of something or a holy hazmat suit to traverse the world without fear of contamination. You need to shatter the glass and figure out how this shocking message fits in the world where we actually live.

Weed Eaters and Reality

My friend Jamie lived close to me while my friends Will and Preston lived on the other side of town. We were all juniors in college, and we had plans to get together one of the first Friday nights of the summer to avoid boredom. When Jamie and I met, we tried to call Will and Preston to get together, but they didn't answer their phones. Twenty unreturned phone calls later, we talked to Will's mom who told us that the two of them had gone camping for the night, two hours north.

When I told Jamie, he gave me a mischievous glance and asked, "Are you thinking what I'm thinking?" Jamie was famous for bad ideas, so my response was, "Depends on what you're thinking."

"You should call Will's mom back and get directions to where they are camping so we can drive up there and scare the death out of them," Jamie said. I liked what he was thinking. We went by Jamie's house to pick up supplies from his garage to scare them. We didn't have a plan, really. We were grabbing tennis rackets and golf clubs, a can of WD-40, an American flag, and other random stuff. Then Jamie grabbed a Weed Eater. The tennis balls made some sense, but a Weed Eater?

Jamie looked like he'd just stepped out of *Lord of the Flies* and said, "A Weed Eater in the middle of the night sounds a lot like a chainsaw."

It was midnight at this point, but we stuffed everything in the back of his Isuzu Rodeo and made the two-hour drive. It took a while, but once we found them, it was beautiful, the perfect ambush. They were thirty yards away. We could see them perfectly, and they couldn't see us. I think God wanted us to scare them, the moment was so ripe.

Jamie was nearly possessed at this point. He started shrieking, and I started throwing tennis balls. Will and Preston started looking around timidly and huddling together by their fire. We couldn't hear what they were saying, but I bet they wondered if Roger Federer had gotten drunk and stumbled into the woods for tennis practice.

Ten minutes later, with no real plan, Jamie and I began to think of new ways to escalate the situation. Jamie all of the sudden screamed at the top of his lungs, "You are going to die tonight!" This is where things turned south.

What we thought was a camping trip for our two friends wasn't a camping trip at all. It was a hunting expedition. They had guns with them. So when they heard, "You are going to die tonight," they screamed back, "We have guns!" *Great*, I thought, *we have a Weed Eater*. But after a two-hour drive, this was no time to surrender, and we fired up the Weed Eater.

After a few moments of the grumbling and roaring, they began firing shots off into the woods. I was hunkered down behind a tree wondering if I was going to make it. After what felt like forever, we finally surrendered, revealed ourselves, and drove home. They didn't speak to us for two weeks.

What was amazing is that because these guys couldn't see, they felt in danger. In reality, they were much larger, and their guns were far more powerful than one Weed Eater, though not as effective for landscape maintenance. They could have killed us in a second. It would take hours to "trim" them to death. But the illusion was far more powerful than the reality.

• • •

The message of Christianity is about leaving an illusion and joining a reality. It is *not* about leaving things that are secular to embrace things that the church has deemed sacred and safe to use. The message of Christianity is about leaving a lie to embrace the truth. To leave darkness to embrace light. This is the journey that Jesus—the light of the world—takes us on. To cross from death to life. Christianity is about leaving things that aren't true to understand things that are.

The first step of believing in Jesus, mentally ascending to who he is and trusting in his resurrection, is the most important step we can take. It is embracing the biggest reality. But it doesn't end there. We keep stepping out of illusions and into reality. Have you ever noticed that churches are often filled with those who sing the right songs and attend regularly but are never transformed? We don't need more of the sacred. We need more of God's reality. It's possible to be living in the depths of the fishbowl but to be trapped in illusion. Because the journey that began two thousand years ago wasn't to become more sacred. It was to walk closer into what is true.

The world doesn't need more people emulating dictums of the church by-laws. The world needs more young men and women who are modeling a journey from death to life, who have found someone to show them how to know reality in a complex world. The beautiful message of Jesus is not about changing the presets on your car stereo, wearing clothes with bumper-sticker messages, or pouring your evil mouthwash down the drain. The beautiful invitation is to become a more alive version of yourself through the truth of the gospel. And to be alive, we have to walk away from whatever lie is holding us captive and toward whatever truth can set us free.

THREE

PAINTING OVER THE *MONA LISA*

DRIP ART VERSUS SKETCH ART

have always loved art. I have never been good at creating it, but I admire people who can. In art, there are lots of different kinds, but it really boils down to two. There is art that you can tell what it is and then there is art that you can't. Art that you can tell what it is—something like the *Mona Lisa* or a sailboat that looks pretty—can be called "sketch art." The artist many times has sat down and planned before he started. Then there is that art that no one really knows what happened. It is as if someone threw a few buckets of paint on a canvas and then put a price tag on it. This can be called "drip art." I don't know why, but I have always liked this kind better.

Sketch art seems like the way a lot of people relate to Jesus and religion in general. There is an exact, polished product that we should go for, and the lines are clearly drawn. When you begin following Jesus, you should begin knowing exactly who you want to become—a good person, who doesn't smoke or sleep around but chooses to be good. Doesn't that seem to be the end goal of faith at times? And doesn't Jesus seem as if he is the one who is the picture and he is the one we should look like?

Is this really what Jesus came to do? To sanitize us? To make sure we have the right friends, the right beliefs, the right habits, and the right moral compass? And if this is the end goal, isn't the standard of spirituality less about searching and struggling, and more about conforming?

Religion often forces us to live our lives like sketch artists, much like the Galatian church that Peter and Paul argued about. Some of us know that strain of trying to fit in and the pain of realizing you can't or don't want to. Eventually the rigid categories break down when life gets complicated. What happens when a teenage couple who knows right from wrong has sex in the heat of passion? And what happens when that teenage couple gets pregnant? All of a sudden they don't fit into the picture they are told to emulate. They don't just have a baby—they have a dilemma.

I have watched this happen with a lot of pastors and ministers. They have spent their whole lives painting and drawing inside the lines, telling people how to draw inside the lines, and all of the sudden they have an affair. What do they do? They painted outside the lines. Aren't they supposed to know how to be good artists? Usually the teenage couple and the pastor chunk the nice clean painting. It is no longer their reality. Instead of picking the brush back up, they believe they can't fix the mess they made.

When the fishbowl shatters, it forces us to become drip artists. Sometimes things happen that you didn't intend to. Sometimes outside forces, maybe a divorce, cause a messy drip. Sometimes we are the ones who knock the paint can over and make the mess ourselves. To approach our spiritual journeys as sketch art is to assume that once we place our faith in Jesus, we are to become more spiritual and less human. To approach our faith as drip art is to assume that we are still quite human. And human beings make messes.

God knew there was going to be a lot of spilled paint down here. He created us as humans, and humans fail. Humans make choices that they regret. Your sense of abandonment and the wandering it led you to has no doubt taken you down pathways that you wish you had not taken. You didn't know why at the time, but abandonment stings, causes an ache, and forces you to wander toward people, places, and things that often leave you feeling more abandoned. Even if your parents could win awards for their parenting, this internal ache is in most of us. While we must ultimately own our choices and consequences, we have to recognize the source of our downfalls in order to heal them.

Abandonment has shaped us, influenced our actions. Seldom do we realize it is the root cause, and neither did the church we grew up in. Perhaps you were told to stop doing certain things and start doing other things, but you never felt *understood* by your faith community. Everything was merely proscriptive and didn't walk you further into God's reality . . . just into a set of accepted behaviors and choices. You were told what to *become*, but no one tried to understand how you *became* who you are. Perhaps this is why you felt guilty for all the spilled paint in your story. You are a drip artist living in a sketch art world. It isn't that you no longer believe. It is just that you don't have the tools to make sense of the messy picture you made.

The Scriptures are full of people who kept kicking the paint can over. And somehow God manages to take the canvas with all of its ugly spots and turn it into a beautiful story. He somehow has the ability to reconcile this human side of us with this spiritual side of us. He encourages us to pick up the paintbrush and keep going, even when we think the mess is unforgivable. He doesn't force us to paint over the mess either. He allows things to be ugly. He doesn't work around reality—he works with it. Somehow he sees a way to redeem it and make it into something different than we imagined. And somehow he makes every painting beautiful in a unique way.

Steps, Not Leaps

I was on a plane ride recently sitting next to this girl who was on her way home from seeing a guy, and she was wondering if she could keep seeing him. Eventually the conversation turned toward careers, and she asked me what I did for a living. "I am a pastor of sorts, I guess you could say." This is always a conversation killer, depending on how you look at it. In this instance, instead of her putting on headphones or staring a hole into her 3.5-ounce cup of soda, the conversation turned toward faith and spiritual things. This becomes the conversation where people start talking like a patient, and I am a doctor. They describe their bumps and aches hoping that I have a mild prognosis, that they have nothing to worry about.

This girl was different, and I admired her honesty. She said, "I could never become a Christian because I could never stop smoking and having sex." I didn't know what to say, actually, I was so dumbfounded. Even in her courageous vulnerability, I think there was a deeper subtext than her confession of cigarettes or one-night stands. Here's what she was also saying: "I have this interpretation of what Christians are, and I don't see myself as one of you."

This girl is like many of us. Her experiences, struggles, and pain have shaped what she thinks about God. She refused to step around the reality of her life and try to become something she wasn't. Perhaps you would tell your life story in a similar way. You would rather be condemned by your parents' faith than lie to yourself or everybody else about who you are. It's a very moral reason not to be moral.

If there is one thing that is true about your story and mine, it's that we've had our share of failures and drips. We haven't come through our abandonment unfazed. All of us, from all different backgrounds, seem to share the same bruises. At first our world gave us those wounds. A traumatic experience in school or at home. A harsh word from a pastor. A moment when you blamed God for not coming through. Whatever the initial cause, eventually we begin to bruise ourselves with our actions and choices. And we do it knowingly. We all know we have done things looking for happiness or a sense of belonging that may be morally wrong, but the short-term benefit outweighs any long-term damage. It is a trade most of us have risked. If we assume that whoever is up there doesn't like messes, we either spend our lives avoiding him, or we spend our lives in a cycle of guilt trying to repay him.

This girl on the plane decided to avoid him. She didn't fit the picture of a Christian. She didn't paint inside the lines. But what if a paint-by-numbers picture isn't the goal? What if painting inside the lines isn't the point?

Step Artists

When God begins walking with someone into reality and out of illusion, he does it slowly. In the Old Testament, God gave the people of Israel the Ten Commandments. These were ten things that would help them live in step with reality, because they were making—and would continually make—a mess. Of those ten, his first rule was not "change everything about yourself." His first rule was "have no false idols." In other words, let's start by not worshipping things that aren't there. When you do that, we will take the next step together. As the Ten Commandments unfold, they get more specific in how to live in tune with reality.[1] God understands human nature better than we do. We don't change overnight—it happens slowly.

One view of the Christian life is that it's a giant leap into something foreign. If your relationship to faith and religion has been strained, perhaps it is because you were made to feel guilty for not leaping far enough. You were told you have to follow Jesus and, from that moment on, conform to a pre-painted picture. The problem is that we all come to Jesus in different ways. We have all been broken in ways that are unique to us, and we all begin asking spiritual questions from different points too. If we all begin from different points, why are we all supposed to end up the same? Why does it seem that before we label ourselves Christian, we have to subscribe to the same beliefs and the same actions in order to fit in?

In the sketch art view of Christianity, Jesus stands at the church doors braced with a fire hose to spray us clean and makes us the same before we continue on the path. That's what it feels like in the church at large—we should be seeing some Christian shampoo and body wash anytime now.

The Christian faith is not about conformity to one another but about learning to step slowly, from right where we are with all our messy splotches. In the Bible, Jesus had many interactions that demonstrate this. One lady reaches up and grabs the cloak of Jesus because she is sick and thinks he can heal her. This is her introduction to Jesus. He doesn't heal her and force her to sign a statement of belief about what happened. Another man is rich, and Jesus tells him he has to give away all of his stuff. This is his entry point.

During his time here, Jesus assembled a band of people to follow him, and they came from all walks of life. The qualifications were not prerequisites of behavior and beliefs. On this path were prostitutes and beggars. The only qualification for this ragtag group of misfits seemed to be feet . . . and a willingness to go. Jesus understood the brokenness of life and showed us this through the people who drew close to him. This kind of understanding, acceptance, and empowerment is exactly what we've been longing for from everyone else. It has the potential to free us if we let it. Like the people of the Bible, we simply need to take the next step with him into reality.

Trust me, every step out of illusion into reality will be different. Your step into reality will be different from mine and vice versa. Whenever religion forces you to forego who you are and where you are, choose to trade that pressure for a walk with God into his reality. I have spent the last ten years of my life working with high school and college students. One of the things that I notice over and over again is that in a group of five people, everyone is in a different place.

I used to meet with a group of high school guys every week. One guy wasn't so sure he wanted in. I think the only reason he came was that I bought him food a few times. One guy had been going to church his whole life yet struggled to forgive his dad who had abandoned him. One guy spent his weekends drinking enough to paralyze a baby elephant and was searching for a new high.

For the guy who didn't buy the whole "Christian" thing, the next step for him was to admit that something beyond us might be involved with everything inside and around us. His next step was admitting there might be a God. For the guy whose dad abandoned him, the step into reality meant turning loose of bitterness that was eating away at him. He already believed there was a God. So each week we met, and we focused on the steps toward reality that we should each take.

Now, if each week I tried to convince the guy who didn't believe in God that he should stop partying, forgive everyone he was mad at, stop sleeping with his girlfriend, and sanitize his whole life, that would be a leap he couldn't take. What if I tried to convince the guy who had a hard time with his dad that he should believe in God? That was a step he had already taken. So we would simply talk about life and celebrate the steps we could take and not worry about the next one. Maybe the Christian faith isn't all about leaping and sweeping changes—maybe it is more about taking step after step. Maybe that girl on the plane shouldn't worry about whether or not she quits smoking yet. Maybe she should begin with considering that God is more than a naughty and nice list, that he's a God who created and holds reality. He can be known like a person and can show her the truth about her life. When conforming isn't the goal, the pressure to leap is removed. Only then can we begin stepping toward reality.

The journey of leaving illusion for reality is not an easy one. For example, control is an illusion. The belief that I can control whether or not I take my next breath is false. We have no control over anything, really. Leaving the illusion that I can control people and things is a step in the right direction. Let's try a different one. A friend of mine recently told me he was a sex addict. He had tried to deny it and act like nothing was wrong, but he couldn't deny it anymore. His honesty was about more than admitting a problem; it was about leaving an illusion that things were fine and embracing a reality that they weren't.

We all buy into lots of illusions, don't we? We deny certain realities about our lives, and we embrace illusions because they are easier than confronting something difficult. If we drink until we get drunk, we do so because it feels much better than reality. The boom of the drug culture is built on this premise. Illusion is better than reality. You can snort or smoke something and go somewhere that gets you out of here. For a little while anyway.

Money is built around illusion too. Money tells us that

if we have enough of it, then we can control our destiny and build our happiness. Most of us would admit that is not true. Jesus doesn't invite us to leave these things behind because they are bad—*he invites us to leave them because they are not real.* In other words, a life spent honoring the commands of Jesus isn't about morality. On deeper levels, it is about reality.

A genuine Christian spirituality is about discovering what is real when everything else isn't. The spiritual quest begins when we assume something we can't see is more real than what we can.

Along our spiritual quest, we begin to discover certain truths that aren't tangible but are somehow real. If that is true, and it possible to walk into some things that we can't see but are real, it is possible to walk further into illusion too. For the girl on the plane who told the story of not wanting to stop having sex, she eventually will feel that a piece of herself is given away to it. It becomes an addiction that she has to feed. The more she feeds it, the more the addiction grows. Eventually this addiction becomes her. All of a sudden, something tells her deep in her soul that this is about more than just sex. It is about something having control over her that she cannot see.

Perhaps you relate to her. Perhaps her story is yours. Should she forsake her ways and sign herself over to new rules? What about you? Perhaps that seems like the only option. What if you have the option to leave something that is not real for something that is? That is the path Jesus offers, a path that leads to something that is real. For us, the journey is not about sanitizing ourselves; it is about a journey to reality. If we leave behind the illusion of love and happiness found in one-night stands, that is a step in the right direction. If you find yourself in a marriage to a loving and committed spouse, then that is experiencing love in its most real sense. It may be a harder path to walk, but it is a better path to walk.

Choosing Confusion

That path is about stepping from a faith of right answers to a faith of right questions. I have a friend who has wrestled with faith his whole life. He thinks Jesus might be real, but he doesn't think about faith in the same way that I do. His objections always focus on whether heaven and hell are real places. He doesn't know if he can believe in a garden where God set up Adam and Eve to fail, either. He always wants to argue about those things with me, and I try to give him answers to some of his questions. To be honest, I don't really think a person's salvation is contingent on whether or not he knows.

What if he doesn't have to know? What if none of us really know? What if he can allow his questions to stay questions? Why can't faith be faith? Am I supposed to tell him those questions are wrong? Many of us were taught that passionate faith equals unabashed certainty. We assume that people who fit into the sketch art are people who know all the answers. Perhaps they aren't people who know; perhaps they are people who are afraid of saying, "I don't know."

To ask questions about God and be suspicious of anyone or anything that pretends to have all the answers is a spiritual act itself. Questions can cause messy drips, but they are honest. When we stare at the canvas as drip artists, we are free to ask needed questions and release superficial certainties. Questions are a tool for us as we step toward reality. They place us in a position of learning and searching, making sure we don't fall prey to illusion.

I am envious of my friend. He doesn't have the burden of feeling so certain about everything he thinks and believes. Why do I carry that burden? Why do I get so scared to not know? Shouldn't a follower of Jesus still be asking questions? After all, if we don't ask questions, how will we discover where we should take our next step?

FOUR

THE MYSTERY
OF MISERY

FINDING FORWARD

My wife and I moved from Orange County, California, to the Atlanta, Georgia, area several months ago. I was born and raised on the outskirts of Atlanta, and I moved as far away as I could when I graduated from college. I have traveled quite a bit, even made a home in California for five years or so. But as author Pat Conroy says, "The South's . . . permanent press and it doesn't wash out."[1] Life in Atlanta, like anything, became too familiar. I guess that is why I had to leave. Eventually, though, what pushed me away brought me back. When we moved to the Atlanta area again, there were old friends to see, places to visit, and connections to reestablish. My wife and I were both transplants in Southern California, but she is originally from Chicago. For me Atlanta was a return to the familiar; for her it was just another new place.

Upon our arrival I quickly realized that just because I knew someone ten years ago didn't mean I was still going to know him or her. I guess it's a bit like childhood: you can grow up on the same street as someone, and play in the same sand pit, but that doesn't mean you are going to even speak to each other in high school. Upon my re-arrival, I realized the reason why so many friendships that I look back on fondly had faded.

I lived on the West Coast for five years, and a lot changed in my life. I went to get a degree that was supposed to take a couple of years. I came home five years later with a wife and a dog—and no degree. But life changes everyone. When you run into a person on the street, you may be bonded by a history, but you are separated by thousands of memories and stories since. Perhaps our friendships end and drift apart because it gets so exhausting to tell those stories and memories to people. As I've tried my best to reignite old friendships, I've found it's really a matter of retelling my story. Friendships don't fade because we stop being around people or we get mad at them; they fade because we stop sharing stories with one another.

I am a bit of an introvert, and telling and retelling doesn't come naturally. It wasn't until I got married to an extrovert, and I watched her gracefully execute conversations while I fumbled for words, that I fully realized my deficiency. But am I defaulting to introversion as an excuse? Yeah, I probably am. Part of my trepidation in friendships is the risk involved. My wife and I have had several dinners with my "old friends" since arriving in Atlanta. In our postgame debriefs, she will wonder how I could be so uncomfortable with someone I knew so well. I have a suspicion you know that feeling too. You walk away not sure how you used to be so close. In my case, the awkwardness always comes with guilt, as if somehow I'm not doing something right.

If you are anything like me, you go through seasons where connecting with God seems like running into an old friend. I bet when you talk about God, you find yourself thinking and saying things like, "I used to feel close . . ." or "I used to love singing, but now . . ." In the same way, when you run out of words when you see an old friend, you feel a bit guilty for not knowing what happened or why you're so bad at it.

Perhaps the guilt we feel about a strained or distant relationship with God is a false paradigm, a feeling of our own creation. In religion we were made to feel guilt because we weren't spiritual enough. But if you feel that guilt at all, it is because you are deeply spiritual. Your guilt doesn't come from not wanting to connect with God; your guilt is coming from not knowing how. Your guilt arises from a lack of tools, not a lack of desire.

Don't Tell Me 'Cause It Hurts

A few years ago, there was an article that released excerpts of Mother Teresa's journal, thoughts that she had kept private until her death. One excerpt read,

Where is my faith? Even deep down . . . there is nothing but emptiness and darkness . . . If there be God—please forgive me. When I try to raise my thoughts to Heaven, there is such convicting emptiness that those very thoughts return like sharp knives and hurt my very soul . . . How painful is this unknown pain—I have no Faith. Repulsed, empty, no faith, no love, no zeal . . . What do I labor for? If there be no God, there can be no soul. If there be no soul then, Jesus, You also are not true.[2]

My first thought when I read this was shock—followed by relief. I think Mother Teresa felt what a lot of us feel. We are told to have unbridled certainty in a God we can't see and be impervious to any second-guessing. Usually we just march through our doubt. If we're really self-aware, like Mother Teresa, we will write it in a journal and then try to move past it. After all, doubt is a messy drip. And we don't really know what to do with it, but we are pretty sure it threatens the harmony of religion so many are trying to protect and sustain.

Many of us were taught that doubt is the enemy of faith. After all, can you doubt in a God while you pray to him? Can a Savior that you question the existence of still forgive you? The other day I had a conversation with a mechanic who said he wishes he could believe in Jesus but doubt overcame him and he doesn't know how. Later on, I was flipping through the channels and saw a pastor on TV who was talking about how God had answered his prayers and strengthened his faith. Truthfully, I don't know who is being more honest.

Perhaps doubt isn't the enemy of faith. Perhaps it is just the enemy of religion.

Maybe doubt leads us closer to reality. We are at our most vulnerable when we are asking questions. When we have shunned certainty and know that we don't know, we are open to discovering God's reality. In the pursuit of reality, doubt is a tool for us, not a weapon against us. It gives us the ability to learn new things and step further into truth as opposed to just defending something we are still trying to convince ourselves we believe.

I am trying to wrestle with my own doubt, and I am beginning to realize it has been locked away for a long time because I never saw it as a virtue. But if I say doubt is a bad thing, then I have to say ignorant acceptance is the goal. Perhaps this is why many churches are built around reconvincing the congregation of something they already believe. Nobody says "amen!" to authentic doubt. Perhaps this is why it feels like we have to tune out our deepest thoughts to enter the fishbowl. Or we hide them in a journal. After all, what do you do with doubt?

In the same way faith and doubt are connected, pain and disillusionment are connected. From the first blow dealt in life, whether a death, a divorce, or a sadness over change, we have a hard time understanding why God doesn't seem to make it his goal to make us happy and comfortable. Yet, somewhere along the way we were convinced we were God's top priority, our comfort his greatest goal. When the blow comes—the sting—we don't have a compartment in our minds for it. It doesn't fit into a category.

God stops making sense because we equate him with fulfillment, not hardship. Times where we skate through life unchallenged and confident, this is when God makes the most sense. But a life open to real pain feels separated from a God who doesn't fix it. After all, we are told he can. But we don't know what to do with the disillusionment that comes and the lack of answers when he doesn't. Most people I know who walk away from faith don't walk away because of doubt. They walk away because of pain. Perhaps they don't walk away from God. Perhaps they walk away from the religion that doesn't have room for their disillusionment.

While we aren't sure what to do with doubt or disillusionment, we aren't sure what to do with dissatisfaction either. Certainty convinces us we are on the right path, and we don't know what to do when we realize we don't really like the path but are convinced it is the correct one. We might have a degree of satisfaction knowing we are going to go to heaven when we die. Beyond that, we often find ourselves disconnected from our beliefs because they don't seem to deliver what they promise.

We are supposed to be happy when we love God, not

trudging through and feeling as though we are obligated to our parents or struggling to relate to the very God who loves us. While we believe that love transforms, faith is real, and God does amazing things, we often grow more dissatisfied when we hear stories of it in someone else's life while we remain empty-handed. Didn't we do it right? Is there a formula we missed? I have often felt sunk in my dissatisfaction when I realized how happy faith makes someone else.

Doubt, disillusionment, and dissatisfaction weren't mentioned when we signed up to follow Jesus. This is why, when we take a turn toward the vulnerable, we are left stranded. Doubt, disillusionment, and dissatisfaction are a toxic formula, a street drug taken furtively in a dark alley, a certain precursor to our fall from grace, but it is really just our fall from a fishbowl.

Statistics say that most people come to faith before they are thirteen and that most of those people walk away when they are eighteen. That's astounding. Most people sit in church, hear the message of Jesus, a message that shocked the world two thousand years ago, and what do they do next? They walk away. When did the message go from shocking scandal to status quo? In my experience, you probably don't struggle with doubt, disillusionment, and dissatisfaction because you refuse to believe the message of Jesus is true. No, the struggle is because the way it has been translated to us in church isn't honest.

Hello, My Name Is . . .

While I know the trend of late has been to dismiss Paul in favor of Jesus, we can't forget Paul. As I said before, Paul's work of recasting the message of Jesus for the Galatian culture shouldn't be a one-time thing. It should be a recurring trend when Jesus collides with a culture. Paul's work should continue.

With the right shape to it, the gospel can become woven into the fabric of your life. I don't believe you want to walk away from God. I don't think doubt, disillusionment, and dissatisfaction are the death knell you think they are to your faith. The Christian story just needs to be retold to you.

When I was a kid, missionaries came to our church. We prayed for them, gave them money, and sent them off to a country to share Jesus with people who had never heard of him. This was a beautiful thing. I remember teary eyes and loud worship, praise about the *real* work of God in the world. But now I wonder if the mission field isn't people like you and me. People who need a fresh injection of the world's most incredible story told in a way we understand.

I believe a Christian story that allows doubt, disillusionment, and dissatisfaction wouldn't crumble the moment it graduated from high school. I believe if you had been taught that Christian faith was just that—*faith*—your faith story would be different. I believe if you had moments where someone celebrated the small steps you did take instead of pointing out the giant leaps you didn't, your view of Jesus and church might be different. Had the message been about leaving illusion to pursue reality, you wouldn't be reeling right now. Heap on top of that damnation about the things that helped you make sense of the world—movies, music, art, your friends, etc.—it's no wonder the lows have been so low and the highs have been nonexistent. I'm convinced that a Christian story that acknowledges the abandonment of a generation is the honesty we need to restore our confidence in the pursuit of faith. Forget about religion; that's no longer an option.

I don't know where you are in the faith journey. Perhaps you left the path altogether. Perhaps you are hanging by a thread. If you are like me, your story is filled with moments of deep love for God and moments of wondering what it all means. If so, it is not another crack at religion that you need, or even a season of "figuring it all out." You need a reintroduction to the faith you already have.

Old Friend, New Place

When we encounter an old friend, we can either go through the motions, or we can genuinely, wholeheartedly try again. If we stay rooted in the past, seldom is there going to be a future. We need a shared context, a shared struggle, something that unites us in this moment, not something that recalls what did unite us. We need to know that God is in our new, unfolding experiences, that he is a part of our rapidly changing new world, and that he hasn't abandoned us in our time of need.

If you hang around many churches, you begin to feel like God can move in spite of our culture, not in light of it. But a meaningful faith, one that can withstand the trials of life, doesn't force us to neglect our everyday experiences and thoughts. It lives in the tension between citizenship in the kingdom of God and citizenship in your hometown. Somewhere in the marriage of that tension where God's reality resides, guilt can be released. We can be taken out of a crisis we didn't need to be in. And God won't be an old friend who doesn't know what to say.

Choosing Mysteries

When I read the Scriptures, I see few of the people God chose to use possessed superhero talent; rather they possessed just the courage to do what they thought God said they should. If Moses were living and a pastor in my town, I probably wouldn't want to go to his church. The Bible portrays him as someone you wouldn't want to follow to McDonald's, let alone through a desert for forty years. Yet there he finds himself, the leader of the people of God in their shining moment of escape from Egyptian captivity in

Exodus chapter 3. A few pages over, in Exodus chapter 16, the people are about a month into a forty-year journey, and they want to turn around and go back to slavery.

There is an interesting exchange in verse 3 of Exodus 16, where the Israelites say to Moses, "If only we had died by the LORD's hand in Egypt! There we sat around pots of meat and ate all the food we wanted, but you have brought us out into this desert to starve this entire assembly to death" (NIV).

The Israelites knew the promise of God was that he was going to lead them to a land of milk and honey if they would just trust Moses and walk forward. Yet they just wanted to go back to where they came from. They knew that where they came from might have been miserable, but at least it was predictable. They preferred misery.

The journey from illusion to reality is step by step into mysterious places. A part of our humanness draws us toward misery. We have to fight ourselves to take a different path. It's why so many of us get stuck in relationships we don't want to be in, jobs we can't stand, colleges we don't belong at, majors our parents choose, and towns we want to leave. We may be miserable, but misery feels better than mystery sometimes.

I've begun to realize in my own life that my doubt, disillusionment, and dissatisfaction aren't my parents' fault, a church's fault, or God's fault; they are the result of my own inability to step onto a mysterious and different path of relating to a God I've become estranged from. I've begun to realize that my broken friendship with God isn't because my parents got a divorce, it isn't because I couldn't find the right small group to join, and it isn't because the worship is the wrong style at my church; it is because, like many of us, I have wallowed in the misery, ignoring the hope that I could reconnect to God in a brand-new way and in a brand-new place of my life.

As in a relationship with a parent, we can't have the same relationship with God at twenty years old that we had when we were ten. If you try to relate to your mom at this phase of your life the way you did at ten, it would be odd, awkward, and inappropriate. The same is true for God. Our friendship has to change or the relationship dies. We need a new way to connect, a way that might seem mysterious.

If you are going to find your way back to God, you are going to have to leave behind old ways, perhaps ways that might feel safe but ways that have left your soul feeling displaced. As scary as it may seem, you need mystery. You need a new path. Don't turn around. God beckons us to an exciting new way of relating to him if we step forward.

FIVE

HOW TO WRITE
A LOVE SONG

WHY GOD GAVE YOU
AN IMAGINATION

G arth Brooks was the first idol I ever had. He was the first artist who really connected with me. I remember as a kid, every time he released a new record, I would go home and play every song over and over. I would even stop the album and write down the lyrics so I could memorize every word. In retrospect, there is something really funny about a sixth-grader crooning to songs about cheating and drinking beer, but it wasn't about the lyrics—it was about the feeling. Garth just had a way of making you feel what he felt. In a world of posers and wannabes, this was something that was real for me. He felt it. So did I.

I remember my dad taking me to one of Garth's concerts when I was about twelve or so. I felt like I had been to church. If there had been an invitation at the end, I would have walked down the aisle. I used to make my dad take me to country and western stores to buy boots and cowboy hats.

I'm sure he thought this was ridiculous, but it mattered to me, and he was nice enough to play along.

All of us seem to have an experience like that, something in our childhood that grabbed our attention and our parents thought was humorous. We don't really fight it because we want to feel something—and we don't really care what they think. These childhood experiences are important to us because they are the first moments in which our hearts are awakened to what being a fully alive person feels like. We all need something that makes time stand still for us and reminds us that we are alive. If we don't find something to get lost in, somehow we end up lost.

Maybe this is why some people go through life like robots. The first band you loved or the first movie you watched that moved you is something you remember forever. Most people put those childhood memories in a box and store it somewhere at their parents' house when they get older. Some spend the rest of their lives chasing that feeling. To this day, when I get depressed, I can put on a Garth Brooks album and get lost again.

Are We Humans, or Are We Dancers?

While you and I may not share the same musical taste, I would imagine you are just as passionate about your favorite artists. After all, everyone loves music. While the relationship between pop music and the church has been strained in our lifetime and the better part of the twentieth century, there is a spiritual nature to the right song, the right voice, or even the right guitar riff.

For thousands of years, people have enjoyed music, even when there weren't many options. There is something spiritual in it, something emotional, even when we aren't sure what the words are saying. We love to listen to music with other people, whether in a car or in a concert hall, knowing the experience we are having through that particular song is uniting us with someone else. Music has a way of moving beyond our minds, even when our minds don't know what we are singing, and it captures our hearts. Music isn't bound by the words that it sings. It speaks a language beyond the words.

I Still Haven't Found What I'm Looking For

If people are honest, I think they would say that listening to their favorite musician is more appealing than going to church. Why is this? Didn't God create emotion? Didn't God give us a capacity to feel? So why do we have to go to everything but him to feel something? Perhaps you find yourself driving for hours to see your favorite band, or waiting by the computer for the tickets to go on sale, all in the name of feeling the music. The death of Michael Jackson was a powerful reminder to me of how music can impact people. Our fervent celebration, adoration, and mourning would have made an outside observer think that a deity had died. I don't recall the death of a president or king earning the attention that was given to the King of Pop.

For many of us, we stopped working out our spirituality in the church and we started working it out through our choice of songs.[1] If you turn on the radio, the blend of spirituality and music is almost seamless. In the early 2000s, it was bands like Creed, Lifehouse, and Evanescence who had hit songs that could have been and were played in churches. Across the 1980s, 1990s, and 2000s, U2 reached across spiritual space and into our radios with their larger-than-life sounds and lyrics.

If you made a list of your ten favorite songs, I would imagine they would show more than your musical taste; they would chart your spiritual journey. Our favorite bands pick up where our pastors and parents left off. The music we listen to is speaking into the spiritual vortex of our lives. We listen, digest, and insert their lyrics into our worldview.

We live in a world that forces us into histrionics, behaving the way that the atmosphere demands. We find ourselves playing "school," playing "family," playing "work," and perhaps losing a bit of ourselves in the process. Our world has compartmentalized us, and our musical taste is often our expression of who we believe we are, regardless of what the world believes about us. Music puts us back together; it picks up the pieces of fragmented lives and makes us whole again, at least while that song is playing.

Mind Games

I read about a study that surveyed odd places people had fallen asleep: 46 percent of those surveyed admitted to falling asleep in class, 39 percent surveyed admitted to falling asleep on public transportation, 33 percent surveyed admitted to falling asleep while in church, 23 percent admitted to falling asleep at their desk. I draw a lot of conclusions from that survey, but is it possible that the message of Jesus is being conveyed with such a lack of creativity that it is as exciting as going to work or riding on a public bus?[2]

For most people who go to church, it is usually limited to an hour-long experience on a Sunday. Outside of the church, most people understand it as a Sunday-bound activity. The hope is that this hour will change the direction of the 167 other hours experienced in a week. Given such a limited time frame, churches do the best they can to get across as much information as they can. The Bible is filled with lots of words, and churches are filled with a lot of words explaining those words. We all know that a relationship with our Creator is a mystical and transcendent experience, but very few of us would use those same words to describe the last church service we attended. More often than not, it is a lot of words. Some are applicable; a lot of them are not.

And it isn't that all these words are bad. It's just that they are intended for our minds and capture very little of our hearts. Jesus consistently talked to his audiences about listening not just with their ears but with their hearts as well. Jesus knows that our hearts are leading us, not our minds—for better or worse. A lot of the things the Bible says do not make sense when you read them without your heart. This is perhaps why it is so confusing to us when we try to read it or try to wrap our minds around it in that hour on a Sunday.

Jesus did for his audience what Garth Brooks did for me or what your favorite bands do for you. He was the ultimate lead singer, in a sense. When I read stories of grown men dropping nets and dying women fighting through crowds, I imagine how he made them feel, and I bet it wasn't just what he said but how he said it. When people came to hear him talk, they felt alive again, and they felt like something mattered. Those who followed him didn't really care where they were going; they just followed because they felt something. It was about more than words and diatribes. How do we get that back?

One Big Love

It is impossible to study culture without studying the language of that particular culture. In the English language, we have more than two million words. These words combine into phrases we assign to something to give a shared meaning to a particular thing. For instance, if I were to use the word *happy*, it means a general experience that all of us can relate to and there is a shared understanding. Our words are really a way of measuring our experiences. *Happy* communicates a degree of a particular feeling, while *exuberant* gives a larger portion of that same feeling. If I were to say that word to someone who didn't speak my language, he or she wouldn't know what I was talking about.

In Swahili, a language spoken by many tribes in Africa and in places like Kenya, they don't have a word for *future*.[3] This idea that is common to you and me isn't shared there. The average life span isn't that long because they don't have adequate sanitation, health care, or even water. So they don't have a word for something they can't imagine.

When we talk about what it means to be a Christian, I wonder if language does more damage than good. Our language makes things seem like they are understood, when perhaps they are not. For instance, when you describe God, what words would you use? The first word that comes to mind for me is *big*. Doesn't it seem strange that I would use the same word for God that I would use to describe a shopping center?

The second word that comes to mind is *love*. Doesn't this seem strange that I would use the same word for God as I would use to tell a friend how I feel about her new haircut? Aren't there experiences you can't find words for? Perhaps there was a time when you were somewhere with a group of friends, and it was one of those moments you got lost in because it was so enjoyable. And perhaps there was a time when you tried to tell that moment to someone else, and you really couldn't. You just had to say, "You had to be there."

In our attempts to put language and words on faith, so that it will make sense in our minds, we have really taken something that means more than words can contain and made it seem less meaningful. So much of our faith is based on using the approved words and phrases to describe it. Our faith becomes a publicity release or talking points sent down from the higher-ups instead of a truth we safeguard in the depth of our souls. For instance, the phrase *relationship with God* communicates way less than the experience can contain. English simply doesn't have the capacity to describe what that feels like in reality. Perhaps we think we must understand everything with our minds and must have the ability to express it in our language to verify its credibility. But is this true? Did Jesus intend for his reality to be perfectly bound up in our understanding? Maybe faith should feel like a song that makes you get lost in the feeling even when you don't know the words.

Perhaps in our attempts to explain God so we can grasp him with our minds, we lose the ability to communicate to the heart. Maybe this is why people leave church, and their minds are full of stuff to know and stuff to do, but somehow their hearts are still empty. Perhaps what you and I need in our Christian faith is to feel deep in our hearts that someone believes in us, not a bunch of truths that we should believe in. Young men and women keep going to everywhere but church because they aren't looking for the right words and phrases, they are looking for something deep in their hearts that makes them feel like they matter.

When we live in shallow religion, our hearts and minds end up in different places. One grows and learns, while the other one gets cold and dies. So how do we talk about faith if words do damage to it? How do we talk about Jesus in such a way that invites our hearts along too?

If God's goal is to take us from illusion and move us into reality, then we have to move beyond our minds and into our hearts.[4] We have to allow God into the places that our favorite songs go, transcending our minds and giving us something to feel. If God longs to awaken us to his reality, we have to begin with an understanding that we can't understand. His nature and his way are foreign to us, and all of the words and phrases we can use don't really measure him and what it means to interact with him.

Perhaps this is why Jesus didn't communicate in catch phrases and bumper sticker banter—he used pictures and metaphors. Where words are legal and descriptive, imagery is spiritual and organic, like the language equivalent of sketch art versus drip art. Jesus was often asked what he was trying to do or who he was, and he answered by saying he was like something else. Jesus knew that our words fail us. They don't have the power to fully describe what he has come to do or who he is. So why would he contain himself in words? I could spend pages describing what Jesus is like and making sure you agree with all of my assumptions, or I could just draw you a picture.

While words are important, we have to recognize that how we *picture* God in our hearts and minds is more crucial than agreeing with how others explain their experience of him with religious language. I think we get told what to believe about God and the right words to use because the more accurate we can be, the less risk there is for someone to misunderstand or believe in the wrong God. Images leave themselves open for interpretation. Jesus took a great risk. Jesus didn't fill in the blanks. He painted pictures with his words, and he let them speak. He was a master at the art of brevity, whose imagery could transcend any culture's language and speak throughout time and space.

Get Your Head into the Heavens

We like our faith to be reasonable and rational, able to explain in phrases or words, but we do not realize the limits that we place on ourselves by doing it this way. Theologian G. K. Chesterton summarized this thought:

> Imagination does not breed insanity. Exactly what does breed insanity is reason . . . Poetry is sane because it floats in an infinite sea; reason seeks to cross that infinite sea, and so make it finite. The result is mental exhaustion . . . the poet only asks to get his head into the heavens. It is the logician who seeks to get the heavens into his head. And it is his head that splits . . . the madman is not the man who has lost his reason. The madman is the man who has lost everything except his reason . . . materialists and madmen never have doubts . . . mysticism keeps men sane. As long as you have the mystery you have health; when you destroy mystery you create morbidity.[5]

Our words are needed to explain God, but they force us to be rational. Faith is an act of the imagination, not just an act of logic. When I spend my life trying to explain and make sense of God, fitting him into my mind, I feel like I'm going insane. He is beyond my understanding, and the only faculty I have to grasp his nature is not my mind but my imagination and my heart.

I have struggled with depression at various points of my life. Feelings of depression have come and gone in my heart, and they have been a normal facet of life for me.

They happen most often when I am being too rational. Some of the most depressed people I know are the brightest and the most sensible. Being trapped in rational minds while being caught in an irrational world drives us beyond the brink. If we try to reduce the God of all things into our minds, we will go insane. A better path is to get our minds into the heavens.

Imagine All the People

I can remember listening to lots of sermons and memorizing some Scripture when I was a kid. Very little of it do I remember now. All the information I have learned about God sits in some distant corner of my brain like an adult who stores his childhood report cards in the attic. All of that information about God is really important. I admire churches that take seriously the command to love God with our minds. I just think the work of the heart is equally important. To do this, it has to transcend words and become an experience. I don't remember much of what I learned in middle school or high school. I do remember all of the field trips.

Maybe our spirituality should be as much about the experiences we have as the information we learn. When we experience and practice our faith instead of just hearing it, all of a sudden our imagination is given something tangible that it can feel. I can know what forgiveness is and how it works.

I can even know the name of someone I should forgive, but until I experience forgiving someone, it is just an idea. I can know what grace is, I can memorize verses on it, but until I do something wrong and someone grants it to me, it doesn't make sense. The people I know who keep their hearts and minds on the same page are the people who don't just talk about faith, they are people who are rolling up their sleeves and living it.

A while back, I met a fifteen-year-old girl who told me she was going to raise sixty-five thousand dollars to build a well in Africa so people there could have water. She asked me to help her, and I put her in contact with people who could tell her how to do it. About a year went by, and I heard from this girl again, and she had actually done it. There was a passion in her soul and a fire in her eyes that I didn't have. It wasn't because she heard a great sermon—it was because she experienced one. When we study the life of this man named Jesus, we see that he offered people life-changing information. He also offered people a life-changing experience.

We are living in an era when we need something beyond our minds that speaks deep into our hearts. We are hungry to know what we cannot know, striving to find what seems out of reach. When our hearts and minds end up on different pages, it is only our imaginations that can lead us back to unity. Not reason. Jesus isn't opposed to reason, and he was very much bent on practical teaching. But the very essence of his mission and life was about causing us to look upward and to see something with our hearts that our minds couldn't comprehend. He knew that only our hearts could lead us into the beyond, into what is most real. In a world where we know that most of what we can see isn't real, our imaginations are our last hope to understanding what is.

SIX

WHO STOLE JESUS?

THE POPULAR SAVIOR AND
THE UNPOPULAR CHURCH

One of the largest and most glamorous malls in America is about a mile from the church in Costa Mesa, California, where I used to be a teaching pastor.[1] More than a mall, it is a symbol of a posh, glittering, and exclusive culture too. It is filled with Louis Vuitton–type stores and Louis Vuitton–type people who shop there. Across the street sits a much smaller, more run-down building in the shadow of this mall. It has only a few stores, and it proudly displays the name "anti-mall" on its marquis. It's filled with grungy-type stores and grungy-type people who shop there.

I am not quite sure why certain words in the English language sound awful when you say them. The word *institution* is one of those words. If you pepper a conversation with that word, you will sound like a really smart person nobody likes. Over time, words begin to sound like what they are. Everyone has nice thoughts when they hear the word *buttercup*, for example. That word just rolls off the tongue like honey. Perhaps we should trade the word *institution* for the word *buttercup*. I bet Americans would feel less threatened by the buttercup of politics and they would eat fewer Reeses' institutions. Foregoing the etymological rabbit trail, when it comes to institutions, our parents' generation is much like that glorious and sacred mall, and ours is more like the anti-mall across the street.

Sports is one of the great institutions in America that we watch but we don't trust. In the summer of 2007, the three major professional sports in America all found themselves in trouble. In baseball, the marquee slugger of the league was fast approaching the sacred mark of 755 home runs while steroid accusations surrounded him. How was the commissioner of the league going to react to someone who might have cheated? Would Hank Aaron, the former home-run king, be there when the slugger breaks the record? Everyone weighed in with an opinion.

Football found itself in a deeper scandal. Its highest paid, most electrifying quarterback and star, Michael Vick, was under suspicion for dog fighting. Would he go to jail? Would the NFL let him play? Once again, everyone weighed in. Basketball found itself in the most serious of trouble. Tim Donaghy, a referee, admitted to betting on games he officiated. Does this taint the integrity of the game? Did other officials bet? How many people lost money because of his actions? Once again, everyone had an opinion.

While each of these sports institutions scrambled to

repair its image, fans everywhere wondered if they could forgive. Sports are the last in the long line of institutions in America to undergo a major scandal.[2] Politics in our country, on both sides of the aisle, seem beyond repair. It is almost assumed that anything a politician says is not true. Starting with President Nixon, who resigned amid a scandal he cheated in, Americans have been suspicious of the executive branch. Leaders of major corporations, such as WorldCom, Enron, Adelphia, even Martha Stewart, all got led out of boardrooms and into jails for their scandals.

In the previous generation, there was a much more respectful view of institutions. This was before we knew that presidents cheated, CEOs stole, and athletes were more droid than human. Our generation has been far too jaded not to read between the lines, and we read between the lines on everything, convinced nothing can be as it appears. Our response to sports scandal is to create the X-games. A yearly competition held in Los Angeles where skateboarders, snow-boarders, wake boarders, and other various boards are the new sport. Politicians go on MTV to get votes; they even get P. Diddy to bang the drum. When record companies started charging ridiculous prices for albums, we went online and stole their music.

It seems that the moment something becomes a big, organized institution, it is going to fall. But almost every institution starts the same. They all start as good ideas fueled by passion and mission. Baseball got started for the love of a game. But once it became big enough to be an institution, a moneymaking venture, it began to lose its purity. Baseball then became about fighting to keep the institution alive, having more power or money. Eventually they forget why they began in the first place. Most institutions are this way—they lose sight of the original purpose behind it all.[3]

Another reason that institutions fall is because once they get big and they find their place in culture, something rises up against it, something countercultural. If that thing is good enough at being countercultural, eventually it becomes the culture and the cycle starts over. For example, in the early 1990s, grunge music came out of Seattle with a fresh sound, and bands like Nirvana and Pearl Jam got pushed to the forefront. Grunge music was a reaction to the rock-star, big-hair, and big-guitar-riff culture of the 1980s. Eventually, grunge music wasn't countercultural—it became culture itself. This paved the way for the boy band and hip-hop sound of the early twenty-first century. In fashion, this is why my dad and I both wore bell-bottoms in high school. Culture is a tide pool. Everything has a way of coming back around. Once we get tired of one institution or trend, we move on to another.

The Rise of "Religion"

When I drive around a lot of towns in America, it is safe to say churches take up a large portion of real estate. These churches are different denominations usually, and they are different sizes too. There are currently more than thirty-three thousand denominations alone. How did it get this way? What would America be like if only half of those existed? Christianity started two thousand years ago with a group of people who followed this guy named Jesus. And when he died, they believed he got up from the dead, and they began teaching this to other people. Christianity in its origins was about the ideas that Jesus taught, about a new way of connecting with God through what Jesus taught.

As this movement grew and spread, it began to get organized. It first called itself the Catholic Church, and about fifteen hundred years in, it split into another group called the Protestants. That group just kept on splitting. Two billion people later, you have Christianity as we know it. The ideas were radical in the beginning. They were ideas about forgiveness, faith, generosity, and love. If fashion or sports or politics can become institutionalized, religion can too. In America, the church as a whole doesn't feel like ideas we are talking about and believing; it feels more like an institution we have to join. Sometimes Christianity feels like the giant mall on the corner. And we are the anti-mall crowd that refuses to go in.

As we talked about earlier, America and our generation are profoundly spiritual. The divide between the sacred and the secular, however, has given us a false dichotomy. The issues that you find yourself having with church is not a rejection of spiritual thinking; it is a rejection of institutional thinking. We are the sons and daughters of organized religion, shaped in its shadow only to grow up and question its necessity. As you find yourself leaning away from church, I would ask you to stop and question what it is exactly you are leaning away from. Is it the church or is it Jesus? The growing trend is to give a sweeping answer, lumping Jesus into one massive category with the church, but Jesus isn't the church, and the church isn't Jesus.

While our generation has thrown much of the institution of Christianity away, the teachings of Jesus are doing quite well. Dr. Phil comes into our home with a watereddown message on how families should forgive and people can break dysfunction. Al Gore and Leonardo DiCaprio tell us we should care about the planet. Oprah, who borders on deity herself, amazes and inspires us with her generosity. Bono tells us to care about the poor. Maybe our culture heralds them as saints because they stole Jesus' message. And it is not that Christians are no longer involved, it is just that they are no longer the ones defining what it means to live out the gospel message.

Jesus has come out of the institution and his teachings about morality and poverty are quite popular. Our culture loves his ideas, and they even do them, perhaps better than we do. Recently I went to a U2 concert.[3] It was half rock and half preaching. As Bono talked and sang, he gave a pitch for Africa, and he got thousands of concert-goers to sign up to help the poor. When did rock stars get a conscience? And when did they begin to do a better job than preachers of getting people to do what Jesus says?

And if they stole Jesus, how do we steal him back? Or should we? Or did he just get tired of the institution too?

Church leaders and Christians all over the world seem to know that there is a problem. But they can't decide if the problem is with culture or with the church. To be honest, your answer to that question can depend on how old you are. Younger people say it's the church. Others bent on bloating the institution of Christianity say it's the culture and call on Christians everywhere to engage in a culture war. They tell us we are at war, and we need to fight the decay of society with its evil music and movies. These are usually the ones who get the microphones and go on TV. They call on Christians to fight and to ban and to rally, and this is a message that turns into a shouting match.

I think these men and women are well intentioned. I really do. I like a lot of them personally. I think they remember a time when America seemed like a Christian nation, and they just want it to seem Christian again. They watch young men and women who are angry and hurting create a culture that adds to the decline, and they desperately desire to stop it. But it is possible to be right in a really wrong kind of way. And I think they forget that we are growing up in a world that is different from theirs. And I am not sure if there ever was a culture war, but if there was, Christians lost.

We aren't a Christian nation.[4] None of us who are now being groomed to lead remember a Christian America. We don't remember a time when abortion was illegal or children prayed in school. America is not something we have to reclaim. We aren't going to get it back. People who think we have to fight in a culture war pound their chests and put on battle gear. People who know that Christians lost take off the battle gear and grieve. Things aren't the same. And if we lost, the solution is not to make the institution bigger and to enlarge the army that's already lost.

Death to Life

Walter Brueggemann, in his book *Mandate to Difference*, said the goal of the church is not to prosper; it is that the world may have life.[5] The idea of church is the most beautiful idea in the world. I can't imagine the thoughts rushing through the disciples' heads when Jesus told them about it. But this messy and beautiful creation doesn't thrive when it is trying to reclaim its place in the American framework. It thrives when it is bringing life into death. That simple. It thrives when it is focused on the simple mission that got it started. Why in the world would an institution that has done horrible things throughout the centuries not have been shut down? Because church is still ground zero for God to move.

Even through all the baggage it carries after two thousands years of having flawed individuals involved, millions of people still walk into these buildings week after week because the church, even in spite of everything, is the place where the impossible is possible. Churches come in all kinds of shapes and sizes, colors and creeds, weddings and funerals. But the lifeblood of any church isn't where it lines up in the culture battle or how relevant it is. The lifeblood is always the stories.

If a church is still standing, even if there are just a handful of people left, good stories are there to be told and shared. Stories of God's triumph in their lives. Stories about people surrendering their lives to a higher power, or prayers being answered, or addictions being overcome, or communities being served. Death-to-life kind of stuff. That is something that can't be purchased at any mall—or any anti-mall for that matter. This is when the church is firing on all cylinders. When it is doing the simple work of giving a person or a community a story of moving from death to life.

Perhaps on all sides of denominations and hot button issues we need to remember that all of our bickering and jockeying for position are sometimes simply about helping the church, probably the one we are members of, to prosper. But the goal wasn't for a denomination or a church to have success.

This thing got started so the world may have life. Before the thought of the institution of church even existed, there was this beautiful idea that started to spread in the world. Because a man named Jesus lived and died and lived, death didn't have the last word. What a beautiful message.

Exodus to Exile

If our goal is that the world may have life, then funneling people into an institution is a misguided vision for that goal. In other words, it is not enough to "church" the "unchurched." This line of thinking is based on the idea of a culture war and that we just need to get more people in our camp. In the Old Testament, it wasn't uncommon to find the people of God in one of two positions: exodus or exile. People in exodus are convinced that what they have lost is still theirs and they should fight to get it back. People in exile are the opposite.[6] They are resigned to the loss, knowing they won't get back what was once theirs. I think their story is our story.

God taught his people how to live in exile. In Jeremiah 29:7–8, he tells his people to "seek the peace and prosperity of the city to which I have carried you into exile. Pray to the LORD for it, because if it prospers, you too will prosper." He doesn't tell them to fight it. He doesn't tell them to convert it. Make it better. Engage with it. God knew that his people then had some choices. They could survive there, or they could thrive there.

We have the same choices too. We can lock our doors and board up our windows and hope that our children inherit a different set of circumstances. Or we can roll up our sleeves and help make it better. If we choose the latter, it means we are more concerned with a better world for everyone than we are with a bigger institution. As N. T. Wright so eloquently wrote in his book *Simply Christian*, everyone, Christian or not, longs to see the world "laid to rights."

Wright used this term to indicate the desire for justice that we all have. Even if your relationship to the church has faded, your longing for the world to be "laid to rights" has not. I would be willing to bet you have found a cause to take up, mouths to feed, poverty to decrease, and a way to contribute to the betterment of our world. It isn't a tragedy that the mission of laying the world to rights isn't exclusive to the church. That is a beautiful thing.

• • •

I don't think you dislike Jesus. I think you share his spirit. He was the first anti-mall. I look around and people who aren't Christians are getting involved and feel a sense of responsibility to make the world a better place to live. I think your problem with Jesus is really a problem with the institution that has built up around him. You are passionate. You want to get involved. If Christians led the way to social change, we would not only channel the spirit of our founder but also the world we are in might see us differently. If the exiled church decided to dig in its heels and make this world better, maybe we wouldn't have to wonder why celebrities such as Bono and Oprah are the frontline social revolutionaries.

SEVEN

CHRISTIAN SOUP FOR THE CHICKEN SOUL

THE DEEPEST TRUTH IN THE DARKEST MOMENT

Several years ago I moved to Los Angeles from Atlanta to go to school. Los Angeles made me feel like a child wandering into a movie that was almost complete—I was lost, and I had no frame of reference. There was a family from Atlanta who had a house in the heart of Beverly Hills, and their son was a casual friend I had known back in Atlanta. I grew up in suburban America, but all of a sudden I found myself living in a mansion on Rodeo Drive, with everything Southern California culture had to offer at my fingertips. The mom of this family had her four children out West, and they were all trying to become famous in movies. She needed help rushing her kids between auditions and school. When she offered me a room, I offered to help out with the busy schedules.

A few weeks after being there, the youngest daughter, who was seven at the time, caught a major break and landed a part in a major Hollywood horror film. The daughter and the mom subsequently had to leave for the Midwest for a month while the oldest son and I stayed with the other kids. I became Mr. Mom, doing homework, running errands, fixing dinner, and occasionally washing clothes. Soon after that, when the mom and daughter returned, I moved across town, grateful they had provided a pillow to lay my head on and a family to be around while I got used to being far from home.

I lost touch with the family, but a few months after I moved out, her movie was released. Because I knew it was her big break, I was anxious to go see it. I also tried not to be jealous that a seven-year-old had more earning power than I did. I am traditionally not a fan of scary movies, and I wouldn't go see one unless I had a good reason, so as this movie began playing I moved more and more nervously in my seat. After about an hour, due to my heightened heart rate, I left. A seven-year-old could star in this movie—I was in my early twenties and couldn't even watch it.

There was a time in American culture when movies weren't so horrific and graphic, when films weren't made to shock but to amuse. Our culture is allied with horror films, which doesn't make much sense to me. I understand why movies about sex are popular. And I get why vulgar comedies are popular too. But why do we love to watch something that makes our heart level surge? I understand chasing a feeling, but we would save ourselves a lot of money if we just broke into a friend's house at 4:00 a.m. with pots, pans, and a Weed Eater.

Hollywood makes more horror films than any other type of movie because even if they know it won't do well in America, it will flourish around the world. Scary movies are all the rage in Japan because they are the only films that don't rely on cultural contexts to succeed. For instance, American films reflect an American worldview of love. Comedies require a certain understanding of the cultural setting to make the audience laugh. Chainsaws and machine guns, however, are the same in any language—and they make for big business. How did culture change to the degree where we not only make these movies and go watch them by the millions, but we also put seven-year-olds in them?

If every institution has a worldview, Christianity and film both preach theirs. While the Christian worldview is bent on giving answers to life's toughest questions, the film industry's worldview is about asking more questions. They don't tell us what to think, only what we should think about. Depictions of violence and gratuitous sex are accompanied with deeper meanings about our society. Sometimes even the most sexual or violent films have very powerful messages behind them about the meaning of life.

In the sci-fi film *Contact*, Matthew McConaughey makes a riveting speech and observation about American life. He says, "I think it's because we're looking for the meaning. Where is the meaning? We have mindless jobs, we take frantic vacations, finance trips to the mall to buy more things that we think are going to fill these holes in our lives. Is it any wonder that we've lost our sense of direction?"

Even if you didn't see the film, you can admire his honesty. My hope in the American dream leaves me feeling this way. Most of us have sat in church and heard messages about how to handle the monotony of life. It isn't that we disagree; it is just that speaking the truth doesn't always make us listen. And why is it that we pay lots of money to hear the messages of films when churches give us their message for free?

Graveside Christianity

My parents' best friends owned the big funeral home in town when I was a kid. There was a graveyard behind the funeral home, with what looked like an endless ocean of headstones. My mom and her friend used to meet up at the graveyard to go for walks while my brother and I played football in the graveyard. A few years ago, we buried my grandfather in that same graveyard, pretty close to a spot where I threw an illegal block on my brother when I was seven.

I spent a lot of time at that funeral home. My dad was a pastor at the local church and used to perform services there when people died, usually for people he didn't even know. He used to come home and tell us stories about how hard it was to deliver the final words over someone's life whom he had never met. I have never enjoyed going to funerals. I don't know anyone who does really, but the problem I have with funerals isn't just the sadness of losing someone, it is the answers and explanations given at those funerals explaining away the tragedy that has taken place.

At the funeral of my grandfather, the pastor reminded us several times that our grandfather wished he could be with us but had more important plans. Through my tears, I couldn't help but laugh at the triteness of his explanation. Way to dip into the platitudes.

A friend of mine was telling me about going to a funeral during which the pastor told everyone what great chili the deceased person made. When he had finished explaining how good the chili was, he concluded that God must have been hungry for chili and that is why this man had died. I am sure the grieving widow would have given God all the chili he wanted in exchange for her husband back. I find more peace in the words of Jena Malone's character in *Into the Wild*, when she recounts a funeral scene saying, "People soften by the forced reflection that comes with loss." The film doesn't try to explain the tragedy or put it into a tidy perspective. Whoever speaks the deepest truth in the darkest moment is who we will listen to.

Circumventing Honesty

In *Revolutionary Road*, Kate Winslet's character says in a haunting speech, "No one forgets the truth; they just get better at lying." Perhaps you have found yourself turning on the television or turning to film as comfort because it seems more honest. Our doubt, disillusionment, and dissatisfaction arise from circumventing honesty. While no one longs for the kind of truth that hurts, most of us would rather feel its sting than lie to ourselves. When given the option of superficial certainty or pessimistic realism, we veer toward realism every time. Why is certainty supposed to equate with comfort? As Peter Rollins says, "We must ask whether certainty is really something that brings comfort to the distressed."[1]

Maybe you've tuned out the Christian voices that used to shape your life, but I would be willing to bet that the voices you now cling to, give you the truth between the eyes. Or directly into them. Whatever voice you tune into—on the radio, in film, in music, or on television—someone is taking the filter off and speaking to you. We tune in because we don't want the edited version of life.

True confession: every once in a while when I am watching TV, I stop and watch Jerry Springer. I am always amazed that he finds these people to be on his show, though I suspect it's all staged. As far back as I can remember, he has brought the chaos of transvestites and cheating husbands into our homes. His show's success reminds us that there is always someone out there more messed up than we are.

The funniest part of the Springer show isn't the show, it is toward the end when Springer comes out and concludes with a segment called, "Springer's Final Thought." In this segment he tries to make sense of the madness that everyone has just witnessed, and he offers an Oprah-esque sentiment that always ends with the line: "Take care of yourselves and each other."

Sometimes Christian spirituality feels like Springer's final thought to me. After all the chaos and mess that life offers, we try to cover it with a few one-liners and chicken soup. In our discomfort over the reality of life, we have to make explanations. But do we? Can we let things not be okay? This doesn't only happen when it comes to funerals; it comes whenever we face any kind of difficulty. We always have to remind ourselves and explain to ourselves that there is a silver lining behind every rain cloud.

But is this true? Sometimes there isn't. Sometimes people don't get healed or families don't get reconciled. I have found myself unable or unwilling to keep a straight face when someone of faith explains away pain by talking about how it will one day make sense or one day it will be all right. Certain moments are so unexplainable, moments where the weight of a broken world crushes us and leaves us incapable of spoken words because of what we once had but now have lost.

You know the moments, the ones shattered by the disappearance of something or someone that matters. The moment you know deep in your soul you will spend the rest of your life trying to recover from what you just experienced. The moment where hope is enveloped by darkness. Eloquent words, biblical passages, and catchy phrases seem depleted of an ability they previously possessed. It is the moment where you know it actually won't be okay. We seem to know this, but even that leads us to explain how it will all get better when we get up there.

Is this the power of the message of Jesus? *It may be awful down here, but one day you get to die?* Why do we avoid the reality of pain with triteness and simplicity? Something tells me we do more damage than good when we gloss over pain and paint a picture of a God who makes all things better when the reality is he doesn't. At least not down here. Sometimes there aren't explanations.

Jesus, who died a horrible death himself, didn't deal in pithy comments and trite explanations that skirted gritty reality. He faced them and sometimes he did nothing. He just let it hurt. For some reason, our culture views Jesus as the patron saint of optimism. In a generation of jaded cynics, people who have experienced the violence and pain captured in the movies, there is a bedrock assumption that everything does not turn out okay. We would rather let it hurt than lie to ourselves.

Perhaps this is why we have aligned with the worldview of film when it comes to issues of pain and suffering. Film doesn't try to superimpose answers for pain and hurt; they opt to just let it hurt. When life seems meaningless and empty, the meaning we derive is anchored in the chaos and in acknowledging things aren't okay. Ultimately the meaning is in embracing the reality, not skirting around it. It is the Springer show, without the final thought. Our generation doesn't look for answers in the chaos. Maybe the generation before us wanted answers, but we know that our world is beyond easy comprehension. We are living in functional chaos.

One of my idols in the film industry is Randall Wallace. He is the writer and mastermind behind *Braveheart* and a few other popular films. A while back, I got invited to see and potentially meet him at a small screening in Los Angeles for *Braveheart*, after which he would take questions from the audience.

Wallace grew up in Tennessee and even went to seminary to become a pastor. Through happenstance and frustration, he ended up a filmmaker in Los Angeles. Everyone there got to ask questions for about an hour or so, and he politely answered. Someone asked him what made him want to make *Braveheart* and where he found the inspiration for it. His answer was much different from what I expected. He said he was unemployed at the time he wrote it, and it was the first movie he had ever written. (Not a bad first effort.) He said he was writing television shows that seemed meaningless, and when he told his bosses what he thought, they relieved him of his job.

A few months in, no one would hire him because it was an industry that placed its bets on mindless entertainment, and he solidified his antiestablishment reputation. As the reality came crashing down that he was going to lose his house, lose his cars, and lose his dignity, he sat down and penned *Braveheart*. He then leaned in and paused, almost as if he was going to get choked up. He said that there is something about the chaos, finding a home in it, and letting it hurt that gives you power and a voice. Until you face it, you don't have anything to say.[2]

That was the best sermon I had heard in years.

In a culture that has anesthetized itself with shopping, buying bigger, looking better, only to come up more empty-handed, we need something that is real. We don't need to avoid the chaos, we have to face it. When we choose not to, we spend our lives chasing an illusion that we will be happy if we have or do or appear as the right thing. If we are to have anything to say in the dark moments that reflects a genuine faith, it must come from a place of acknowledging, accepting, even embracing chaos. We try to create our lives assuming that the world is ours and that we can dream as high as we want, trying not to accept the possibility of any obstacle that may knock us off our self-prescribed course. What we lose sight of in this exchange is that sometimes the best dreams are those that happen because of pain, not in spite of it.

Wounded Honesty

There have been many times in my life that I have trusted someone only to have been hurt badly or betrayed by them. All of us probably have. There are people whom I have wounded badly or betrayed too. There have been plenty of moments where life has gotten yanked from under me to the point where I didn't feel like I could go on. There have been moments of despair that have led to me a therapist's couch. Because of the hurt, the loss, the grief, the search for meaning in times that seem meaningless, I have walked through the world with a limp. All of us have one.

It is something that might have crippled us in our families, wounding us deeply, shaping our view of the world and whom we can trust. We can easily point it out in others. It is the girl whose dad walked out and she spends the rest of her life crying out for attention, sometimes literally, sometimes sexually. Everyone seems to know what is wrong but her. It is the guy whose dad had such high expectations of him that he turns into a control freak who can't handle circumstances that fall apart.

One thing is certain about our limps, we all have them and they all matter to us. But seldom do we let other people know they exist.

There is a message that validates our pain and doesn't suffocate it with superficial certainty. As followers of Jesus, our journey is to walk between the optimism of Proverbs and the pessimism of Ecclesiastes. We cling to hope, but we acknowledge reality. We don't cover our limps or flaunt them, but we know that they shape our understanding of the world and our future in it. Doubt, disillusionment, and dissatisfaction don't have to morph into despair—our faith needs authentic voices who don't act as if they are indestructible because they profess faith in Christ. We need to be those authentic voices. We are as human as our nonbelieving friends, and often just as uncertain about why life doesn't work the way it should. Our faith does give us hope, but it doesn't always give us an explanation.

I am trying to get better at showing people my limps. I don't do it with everyone, and it is really hard, but sometimes I have to stop myself in a friendship or with people I work with to let them know they aren't the problem—I have a limp. Usually, they show me theirs. In those relationships where I have gotten badly burned, it is usually by people who didn't show me their limps. They gloss over them with religious language and pithy phrases. I am learning not to trust anyone who doesn't walk with a limp. Eventually those people will hurt you. I don't think they mean to—they simply can't help it. Relationships work better when people get honest, when they stop giving "Springer's Final Thought" to the chaos they have experienced. We bond over our struggles, over the lack of answers, and we eventually confess we are not okay. And the only thing that makes that confession okay is that we both make it.

EIGHT

BODY LANGUAGE

DESIGNER JEANS, TATTOOS, AND TEMPLES

There was a story on the news the other day about a group of terrorists from one country who walked into the mall of another country and blew themselves up. Acts of violence in the Middle East are common, so common that I wasn't even that shocked by it. It was just one of many stories like this that come through our television sets. Young men and women on spiritual missions, willing to die for something they believe in, haunting and impressive.

Immediately following this story, I was bombarded with commercials and advertisements for everything from Viagra and vitamins to pain medication. It is peculiar to me that our culture is bent on preservation and on alleviating pain, and yet there are some cultures where concepts like that are foreign. Do terrorists use Advil? When they get a headache or a cut, would they even use a Band-Aid?

Our religion and our culture shape the assumptions we make about the body. In some parts of the world, the body is merely a means to an end, a tool to carry out a spiritual mission. In our culture, the body isn't about function, it is about beauty and is something to preserve, as if it were an expensive piece of art. We spend billions of dollars a year in America to maintain something that some people in other parts of the world enlist to blow up. So is it that our culture values the physical over the spiritual, and is it that their culture values the spiritual over the physical?

If we come into the world asking questions about it, the body is the house where all those assumptions, observations, and questions live. Our flesh and bones are our first introduction to something real, something that laughs and bleeds, smells and sees; and the rest of our lives are spent trying to figure out what else is as real as our bodies.[1] Our bodies are painful and beautiful reminders of how fragile, weak, and vulnerable we are. We ache when they are bruised, or cry when we watch them lowered into the ground. At the same time, we celebrate and marvel when they are able to accomplish great things—an athlete who can run, an astronaut walking on the moon, and small moments where the body transcends weakness and seems unstoppable.

The Great Divide

My high school had nice cars in the parking lot, most of us wore relatively expensive outfits, and our summers were filled up with stories of lake houses and potato salads. It wasn't a pain-free utopia, but economically we were soaring. Occasionally we would drive into the city to see a homeless shelter, acting more like we were on a field trip than on a mission. We would quickly be whisked away to the comfort of suburbia, usually followed by conversations of how the experience made us feel. The basic summation was that we should all be grateful for our PlayStations and potato salads and grateful that we were born into a different way of life.

Atlanta is a quirky place because eventually all of these seedy elements come north, and when they do, the people with all the money just go farther north. My mom took me to her hometown when I was little. It was really run-down, and I was amazed she had grown up there. Apparently, it didn't used to be that way. It used to be really friendly, and you could raise a family there without a fear, an unlocked-door kind of place. Driving through it now, it seems like a foreign place to my mom, nothing resembling the childhood she had there.

I remember there was this big vote on whether or not to let public transportation into our town several years ago, and no one seemed to want it because they were afraid "down there" would move "up here." Since all the people from up there had lived down there when they were children, they didn't want to have to move up again, so it got voted down. So the rich and the poor kind of play a game, and the poor always drive the wealthy farther up. The rich people try to keep them out, but they can't. I am convinced that one day Atlanta will be in Tennessee.

In church, often our approach to the body looks a lot like my hometown looked. The spiritual and the body are two totally different things; they aren't really one. And we kind of treat the body as if it is the homeless part of town, and the spiritual side of us as if it is where the rich folks live. This leads us to spend our lives trying to make sure the one doesn't destroy the other. We grow up learning and believing that there are certain things that are spiritual, like going to church, serving someone, singing praise songs, or reading the Bible, and then there is everything else we conjecture not to matter.

The body is kind of a problem because it seems to like everything else more than it likes the spiritual. Listening to music, going to a movie, laughing, and many other things feel much more natural for my body than sitting down and reading the Bible or praying. As a result, we begin to think about the body as something we have to control, to get in line with what we know we should be doing. When we put our faith in this system, a good Christian is someone who can somehow separate from his or her natural urges and follow the spiritual ones.

We focus on our minds, feeding them with the right information and truths, and we are never quite sure of what to do with the container of those minds. The body is kind of something to survive the world in, and we aren't supposed to worry about it too much because one day it will pass away and we are, after all, just spirits on our way home to heaven.

Our hope is that one day our spiritual desires will grow and one day the desires of our bodies will kind of die out, and we are disheartened when it doesn't happen. More prayer and principles are the prescriptions for sexual temptation, and we feel guilty when the body still wins. The mind is supposed to be how we teach and train our spirits, and the body is sort of the redheaded stepchild, left alone.

When we do talk about sex, it is mainly about how we shouldn't until we get married, and once we do get married, do we talk about it then? If we do talk about the body, it is through the mind. We never let the body speak for itself, even though it seems to be telling us a lot about what we want. Its experiences, struggles, feelings, and temptations are really uncomfortable topics for most people, so we opt to avoid them to talk about how to pray or how to read the Bible, as if we are on a football team and we need to learn the plays so we can execute them well in the game. Even when our bodies fail us and succumb to temptation, we assume it is because we didn't know the plays well enough and we need to learn them better.

Tearing Down the Wall

In the town of Pasadena, California, there is a freeway that runs through the middle of it, separating it from the north and the south. I have lived on both sides of this freeway, and while it is all part of one town, it is a divide between two different cultures. When I lived on the north side of the freeway, my window was ten feet from the street, and I would often wake up in the middle of the night because homeless men and women would be gathering there. On an occasional Friday or Saturday night, the sounds would become a little louder when my stereo or headphones couldn't drown out police sirens.

I often woke up to the sounds of car alarms going off, which eventually became normal and even soothing, and only once did I wake up to realize that it was *my* car that had been broken into. One time was I awakened at three in the morning to a knock on my door by a homeless woman I had met on several occasions who had followed me and was looking for money. After six months of surprise visitors, broken windows, and little sleep, I moved across town. I didn't have to go very far, just the other side of the freeway, less than a mile from my old apartment, to find peace and quiet. The street that I lived on for a couple of years is south of the violence and noise and is close to picture-perfect. Whenever Hollywood needs a picturesque, middle America set, such as the house used in *Father of the Bride*, they can usually find it here on the glorious south side.

One of the things I love about Los Angeles is that the divide between cultures, economic and racial, isn't as big as it is in other parts of America. It doesn't really exist at all. It is just across the freeway. Somehow, what makes Pasadena beautiful is that it is home to both. Maserati and Bentley dealerships are a minute drive from a place you wouldn't want to drive those cars through. Millionaires in million-dollar homes spoil their children with everything they could ever want while minutes away there is a dad wondering how he is going to feed his. I have never really figured out how or why the people on the north side haven't moved to the south side, but apparently they never have. They don't have to vote every year on restrictions, or even build a wall. Everyone is able to live in harmony together somehow.

I am starting to think about the division between my body and my spirit like the division between the rich and the poor in Pasadena. I mean that to say I am much more comfortable when they are blended together, not relegated to distant corners of myself. I am better at life when I am not talking about myself as if I exist in sections, but rather when I talk about myself as a whole. In a culture where we have been abandoned and left alone to make sense of our world, where we question whether or not we matter or belong here, where expectations and reality are often far apart, the damage that is done to us is more spiritual than it is physical. A dad who has spent more time on his BlackBerry than he has with his daughter doesn't do any real physical damage to her body, but it does somehow impair her soul. The child who watched his mom and dad split when he was nine, wasn't damaged on the outside by the split, he didn't even go through the divorce himself, but his divorce was on the inside.

In a world where a thing that has happened on the inside of us tells us something is wrong down here, the body is the canvas we allow our souls to paint on. It is an outward expression of what is happening on the inside.[2] The body is the way in which we tell the world around us what we think about the world. It is all we have to say about how we feel, our last resort. Fifty years ago, tattoos weren't very common, and neither was body piercing. Fashion choices are no different. If someone wears an outfit from thrift stores and junk marts, it is a way of saying that you don't care about status and you aren't buying the advertising. If you shop at Goth stores, you are taking that statement steps further, saying that not only are you not conforming, but you hate the thought of it. If you shop at American Eagle, it isn't just a brand; it is essentially what you believe you can become, a walking version of the American dream, an eagle that is soaring above the hawks.

A stroll through most lunchrooms in America, high school or college, looking and observing someone's avatar would lead to a thousand assumptions about spiritual decisions. The body speaks. These vulnerable and weak vessels sing songs by themselves, and we get to decide what songs they sing. With the body, there is no divide between what is spiritual and physical, sacred or secular; we are part of a culture that holds the body in high regard. Our bodies are our chance to align the outside of us with what is happening on the inside. We care a great deal about what we present to the world, even if that presentation says we don't care. These flesh-and-bone canvases aren't just physical presentations, they are spiritual ones. We cling to the body, we care for it, work on it for hours; even if we don't, we want to. It is not a means to an end, something to harness for a greater good. Our culture views the body as the end and as the good.[3]

These mortal forms that we care so much about are also telling us about God. He chose to give us these awkward, fragile, weak, and powerful figures. And they speak for themselves. They tell us something about what we want and what we need. We don't just have a body. We are a body. And perhaps we should listen. Perhaps we shouldn't treat them as something that is just to survive and put up with, as if we are more spiritual than we are physical. Perhaps we should let the homeless side of us move in.

The body has always seemed like a utilitarian apparatus, something that will ultimately be my downfall. I hate the thought of dying. I know I shouldn't be afraid of dying if I know where I am going, but I still hate the thought of it. As much as church tells us that death is not something we have to worry about, I think all people of faith are afraid of it. If they weren't, and we were supposed to really think of heaven as our home and not here, then why do Christians go to doctors? Why do we even buy Band-Aids? Shouldn't we ban medicine before we ban R-rated movies and strip clubs? That would be dumb, and so is trying to act as if death doesn't scare us.

It is not even the fear of dying that scares me; the thought of turning thirty scares me. I am terrified of a day when my hair might fall out, when my knees might ache, or even when I can no longer run or ride a bike. But I know it's coming. Every day I walk by a mirror I am reminded that I look a lot like my dad and that I am going to look more like him as I get older. That is really scary when I look at my dad. I talk to him on the phone more than I see him, but every time we get together I see a little more of myself, my body, in his. And then I am reminded that all of the *GQ* magazines, designer jeans, and avant-garde hair products in the world can't stop the hands of fate. He is my destiny. At least physically.

My dad threw away all of his attempts at vanity a long time ago. He is not afraid to go out in black socks, tennis shoes, sweatpants, and a polo shirt all in the same horrible outfit. He doesn't spend money on clothes really. His wife tries to dress him and he hates it. I probably spent more on underwear last year than he spent on his entire wardrobe. If all of the wannabe vagabonds who shop at thrift stores want to look like they don't care when they walk out the door, they shouldn't shop at a thrift store—they should consult my dad. He hasn't been to a gym in years. I don't even think he has seen a mirror in years. And you kind of love him and admire him for it. But as quirky and funny as he is, he is a reminder of my reality. I don't just have a body. I am a body.[4]

The Two Became One

If the promise of Christianity is to make dead people come to life, nothing renders us as dead as division. Nothing makes our souls ache like the pain of being several versions of who we are. Perhaps the Christianity you have left behind is a faith that left you holding your spiritual and human selves at a distance, juggling your identity to fit your environment. I was set on this journey from an early age, believing that the Christian journey should be primarily a moral one.

The movement from death to life isn't a journey to get closer to perfection however. It is a journey to get closer to being whole. Our world is constantly dividing us, forcing us to suppress our homeless side from our rich side so we can gain a job, a grade, a relationship, love, or some other level of status, and all the while we become unrecognizable to ourselves. We know we weren't born this way. Yet we come of age in a complicated world, and the older we get, the more divided we become.

As we move from illusion to reality, we have to move from being divided to being whole.[5] The illusion that damaged us is that we are to move from being flawed to being perfect. Jesus didn't come to make us perfect, and there is no greater reminder of that than the body we possess. A passion for perfection will force us to adhere to a moral code, a code that will lead us into guilt when we fail. A pursuit, rather, of wholeness will help us to reject the divided self, and in the process it will awaken a passion to exist.

Our world is wrought with examples of people who live divided, showing one face in the light only to transform in darkness. We have all done this one way or another, I suppose. The outcome is always the same. Whether on a small or large scale, another part of our soul dies. We become a vacated human, over time going through the motions of the life we have chosen. In this moment, the Christian journey has fertile ground to begin. Jesus enters in to take us from this death we've fallen into, not to become good, but to become whole.

NINE

THE BROKEN COMPASS

BITING THE APPLE AGAIN

A CEO of a rather large technology firm unveiled his company's latest invention onstage. I was awed at his presentation. He was a perfect combination of cool and intellect, and I thought about how much hard work he must have put into his hour onstage. He was so captivating to watch that he could have unveiled a glow-in-the dark spatula and I would have applauded from my couch. For those in attendance, it must have felt like a church service. It even ended with music.

Technology has changed. And it will keep changing. It has advanced to the degree that it is impossible to get through a day without it, and it is advancing faster by the moment. The computer and phone you use will probably be obsolete in less than five years. But perhaps we don't realize that not only has technology changed, it also has changed us.

I have often wondered why the technological advancements of our society have happened so fast, and yet for so much of human history, it all happened slowly. Are we smarter than our ancestors? In my lifetime, I have seen the invention of the personal computer, the cell phone, and the toilet that flushes itself. Yet if you look back over much of human civilization, the wheel is the crowning jewel. Obviously the explosion of information has moved technology along at an exponential rate, but why didn't that happen sooner? It isn't that people have become smarter; it is that our attitudes toward technology have changed.

Leonardo da Vinci is known across the world as one of the greatest painters who has ever lived, but if he had been born in our world, he would perhaps be known best for his inventions. Upon his death it was revealed that he had elaborate drawings of a submarine that he had kept secret. Why? Perhaps he feared the implications it would have on the culture he lived in. His culture looked not only at what an invention was capable of, it also was concerned with the way of life it might undo. Da Vinci's culture understood that technology needs rules, an authority placed over it, so that technology doesn't begin to rule its inventors. In Leonardo's case, this authority was God, and theology, not technology, ruled the day.[1]

From the telescope to the television, inventions alter the course of humanity. For thousands of years, people believed God had interest in mankind on this Earth, and with the invention of the telescope, "the Earth became a lonely wanderer in an obscure galaxy in some hidden corner of the universe."[2] We live in a world that questions the meaning of life because the telescope was invented. With the invention of television, the term "political debate" took on new meaning, and how the world received information changed too.

We have all been born into a world where progress, advancement, and technology have been given a free pass to decide what our lives on this Earth will look like. Most of us will have or do have jobs that weren't even possible one hundred years ago. While our ancestors were citizens of a natural world, we live in a technological one. With every invention, our humanity is altered again and again. Our lives have become cleaner, faster, and longer, but what it means to be in the world is constantly different. We should applaud these inventions; they are marvels of human ingenuity. But we should ask some questions about them too.[3]

The Religion of Invention

Every culture tells a story of what it means to be alive in the world. This story is what defines meaning and purpose, and it sometimes answers questions of what happens to us when we die. In childhood we need to know this story or we end up bored or perhaps destructive. This is one of the chief goals of religion, to give its followers a context for their existence on the planet. Some religions may seem exotic or foreign to someone from another belief system, but all religions are just a story for a group of people. Some stories are really troubling because they center on some guy in Texas who thinks he is divine or focus on a spaceship that is supposedly coming. Both of these are actual late-twentieth-century examples from which we are either handed meaning or we fabricate a story that gives us meaning.

Technology isn't just making our world go faster, it is telling a story too. Inevitably it takes the place of religion— even for deeply religious people. The technological story tells us that there isn't any problem that we can't fix through a machine or invention and that our lives will continue to improve as our knowledge improves. The goal of this particular religion is that we could conquer death and inconvenience with what our minds create.

If there is a problem that hasn't been solved, like death, you could just freeze yourself if you'd like and wait for a solution. Most civilized nations in our world tell this story. With every new gadget we put in our homes and every button we push, we deputize technology to be our savior a little bit more. As Neil Postman wrote, "To every old world belief, habit, or tradition, there was and still is a technological alternative. To prayer, the alternative is penicillin; to family roots, the alternative is mobility; to reading, the alternative is television; to restraint, the alternative is immediate gratification;

to sin, the alternative is psychotherapy; to political ideology, the alternative is scientific polling."[4]

We have been made to believe that technology can save us. One can read the Psalms and see that in times of war, David looked to the heavens for safety. In our culture, we put our trust in a stockpile of highly advanced weapons.

The problem with technology is that, while altering our existence, it is telling a story that is not true. Technology is a broken compass, telling us we are going in a direction we are not. We are never going to be citizens of a death-free utopia. We may be able to make life a little longer, a home a little stronger, coffee a little faster, and a spatula a little brighter, but technology will ultimately fail to produce a cure for death or even inconvenience. Even if it did alleviate both, what would happen? It couldn't answer why we have all been placed on this Earth and what we are supposed to do while we are here.

Our world and the story it tells is bending further toward technology—and further away from humanity. The education system we are placed into as children teaches us how to relate to these machines so we can use them and improve them. We don't learn multiple languages or even much about the history of our world. We ignore our past as we blaze toward the future.

None of this makes us more interesting or more human; it just makes us more efficient and capable of earning a living. Television holds us captive; it becomes a vital source of information, but we have to limit its use, or it will vacate our humanness. If we give it a free pass, it will distract us from our actual life while we "amuse ourselves to death."[5] While our grandparents may not have had cell phones, they didn't have Prozac either. For all that technology has given, it has also taken away.

I don't think Jesus came to teach people how to become Christians. He came to show people what the human experience should look like. If we let him, the red words of Scripture can lead us out of the illusion created by ingenuity and move us closer toward reality. The beauty of Jesus' words isn't just that they offer salvation, it is that they actually make us thought-provoking, fully engaged, inspiring people when we follow them. As we follow the words of Jesus, we not only are leaving illusion for reality, we are also leaving behind a world sold on a false story that empties us of our souls.

Blackberry Muffins

My wife, Rosanna, and I have always had lots of conversations about what types of foods we like. We relate to food much differently. She grew up in a no-artificial-preservatives-or-flavors house, and I discovered my first vegetable in college. When we were dating, she would order fruit salads, and I would order foods that had a catchphrase or a nickname, like the "widow maker" or the "chubby hubby." She taught me about food before we married; in fact, one of my first lessons was to not eat things that the restaurant gives you for free if you finish it.

I didn't immediately understand her way of relating to food. It has taken a long time, but I really believe she is going to help me live longer. One of the things I have discovered is that it is actually really hard to eat well unless you know what you are doing. I have bought books and read articles about what foods to purchase, but I still am unsure of whether or not milk is bad for me, or eggs for that matter.

I don't know why the food industry has made it so hard for us not to kill ourselves; even something that appears healthy can be loaded with chemicals or dipped in Crisco. Perhaps this is the reason why I am constantly meeting someone who is "something-intolerant" and can't eat certain things or take certain medicines. I was in a Midwestern town that boasted of having more fast-food restaurants per square mile than any other place in the world, and right in the middle of it all was one of the biggest hospitals I had ever seen. I wondered if anyone in that town had noticed a connection.

I think the relationship that America has with technology is a lot like its relationship with food. We naively assume that if someone is making it available to us, then it can't be harmful and we should probably try it; and then we end up inconspicuously consuming more. I know I would be much healthier if I were skeptical of something before I ate it, and

I think I would be healthier mentally if I were skeptical of all the devices I have a relationship with too. I am trying to ask some questions of all the technology I am attached to in my life, and while I have discovered much of it does make my life simpler, much of it is quite useless.

For example, I could click a button right now and with a few strokes of the keys inform hundreds of my "friends" what my favorite type of muffin is. Not only that, within a few moments I could probably tell how many of my "friends" "like" the same type of muffin. Maybe that seems harmless, but reading and writing self-indulgent information is for our brains what too many calories is for our bodies.

Gaining Weakness

I read an article that said high school students don't really care about whether or not they get a car when they turn sixteen.[6] I took a moment to mourn the loss of one of America's great rites of passage. The article went on to say that what sixteen-year-olds do care about now is what type of cell phones they have. In our changing world, proximity to actual people is no longer as important as it used to be.

But it seems that while we have more ways of getting in touch with each other than we have ever had before, we are somehow lonelier than ever too. All of these devices are giving us an illusion that we are connected, but in many ways, it is a false connection.[7] This is why it is possible to have more than a thousand friends online and still be lonely on a Friday night. We can spend all day text messaging or talking on the phone, only to long to be in the presence of a real person.

While we are more connected than ever, the reality is that we are actually less connected. While we spend all day in the presence of some sort of device, staying connected to everyone, in many ways it robs us from really connecting to anyone. We maybe have seen a thousand pictures of people we have met, or even become aware of their favorite pancakes, but have we participated in real moments of life with them? That is the difference between watching golf on television and actually playing it.

As we step back toward humanity, perhaps an illusion we have to recognize is that technology doesn't solve our need for connection. We need something deeper. We need something more. We need human beings in our presence who know us, and we need the assurance that with them there is no fear of rejection.

This illusion is hard for me to leave. I like to think that I can stay on the phone or online and be connected. To be honest, relationships don't come naturally to me. I feel really awkward trying to get to know someone, and I am much more comfortable alone. Even when I do connect to people, I like there to be a safe distance. I don't want people to know too much about me. I hate being rejected, and I spend a lot of my life trying to prevent it. Maybe it is because I grew up in a divorced home and something in me always waves a red flag when someone else gets too close, warning me to not get burned.

Sometimes I feel that if no one ever really knows me, I can be admired. If I am known, however, I am afraid I won't be admired anymore. I think we all want to be admired. I want to be admired for being powerful and strong. People may admire me when I am distant and strong, but they will love me when I am close and weak.[8] If I choose to remain strong and distant, then I also give up my ability to be loved by someone—male or female. Perhaps this is why we use technology. It allows us to put up profiles that make us look strong and allow us to be admired; it allows us to think we are socially elite and connected; but it never allows us to be loved. To leave this illusion and enter into meaningful relationships, we have to decide that being loved is better than being admired in our avatar.

Analog People, Digital World

I don't think men one hundred years ago had a midlife crisis. In our culture's fascination with gadgets and more gigabytes, we have also lost the ability to enjoy silence. We now run from thing to thing. Even in the summer, we are lucky to see a vacation. Who has time? But something in us tells us we have to slow down and breathe, that our pace of life is unsustainable.

When we don't listen to that voice, we wake up one day and our minds and our bodies can't seem to be in the same place at one time. We. Become. Fragmented.

I think men who haven't slowed down in years and know something has to give have put us in this modern day crisis. Perhaps this is why things like Yoga classes are all the rave in our culture. We now pay for silence. Starbucks and bookstores are our new centers of community. Sometimes I will drive around in the car with the radio off, and I realize that silence is the loudest noise I have heard in a long time. Not that long ago, I began to realize my mind was so fragmented that I couldn't go to sleep at night. After a day of rushing from thing to thing, my computer could power down, but I could not. The sun would be peeking in my window, and I would still be restless.

I guess I had insomnia. When you have insomnia, as Ed Norton says in the movie *Fight Club*, "you are never really asleep and you are never really awake." Life is just kind of lived in this constant fog. I eventually went to therapy. My eyes were opened to the fact that not only did I not have any meaningful relationships, I didn't have any silence either. I was functioning like a droid on a mission, not a human who needed to pace himself. We all seem to run at that pace. Eventually either our bodies start aching or our minds stop working. Sometimes it is both.

Not only do we need meaningful relationships—we need

meaningful silence. We need periods of time when there is not a cell phone or a computer around, no noise of something buzzing or the sound of a new instant message popping up. Our lives are designed to operate in a certain rhythm, and when they don't, we become our own worst enemy. God designed the world this way. From the very beginning of time, he has ordered rest. He took a day off, himself. I don't think he did it to be cruel, but like a mother sending her child to bed, he probably did it because he knew we don't function well when we don't.

Returning to Where We Came From

In the Bible, when Jesus encounters someone, they always leave different than they came. There is a dramatic example of this in the gospel of Mark. The story goes that Jesus encounters a man who is possessed by a demon, and when Jesus asks the man what his name is, the man replies, "My name is Legion, for we are many."[9] He was actually more than many—a legion is six thousand. The story goes on that Jesus casts all of the demons out of this man, making him one again and, I suppose, giving him back his original name and his identity. It's a powerful story that illustrates Jesus giving someone his life back and pulling him out of the dysfunction that Jesus found him in. Although the man in the story was alive before Jesus met him, he didn't really have life.

Technology does to many of us what happened to the

man in the story. We are alive, but out of touch with what it means to be alive. As I become more and more skeptical of technology, I feel I am becoming one again and reclaiming what it means to be human. I feel like I am stealing my identity back from the story technology is telling. Technology, for all of its benefits, has facilitated so much of the dysfunction and fragmentation of my own life and friendships—it has even clouded what the term *friend* means.

For every gadget we buy and avatar we create, we take a step away from what it means to be alive, and we take a step toward being "many." Followers of Jesus aren't necessarily people who need to move to an insulated land, free from the perils of Google, but they are people who should be coming out of death and into life, out of the natural order of American life, which actually creates so much disorder, and coming out of virtual connections to embrace actual people. When we do, we move away from being "many" toward being one. We take a step closer to being human.

TEN

HAVING FAITH IN FAITH

WHY *MYTH* IS NOT A FOUR-LETTER WORD

The most beautiful parts of life have no formula for happening—they just happen. That is part of what makes them beautiful I suppose. For example, while I was dating, the deepest advice I could ever come across on marriage and love was "when you know you know." It seems to me that if God intended who we marry to play such an important part in our lives, then love should be gauged with some type of device with some degree of accuracy more reliable than "when you know you know." I'd even settle for a professional opinion.

But there really isn't a professional opinion or a gauge, and the only compass through the maze is your own soul. I never really believed that logic about something as life altering as love could be true, which is probably the reason why the day I fell in love with Rosanna and the day I told her that I love her aren't the same day.

Perhaps you have experienced love, or perhaps you are

chasing it. On either side, you have faith that it exists. Love is cast over us from the time we are born. We are told love is what gives life meaning, that it is what we should give to someone special, to our friends, to ourselves, and to our God. Yet no one can really define what love is. It can't be studied, and it can't be understood apart from the one who experiences it.

Life can't be reduced to a series of interactions with people. Life isn't a series of random events or a box of chocolates. Life is a series of moments with people we love, and our souls need love or they die. We all chase it—even if that chase has kept our local therapist in business. We keep chasing it because we believe that a life without love really isn't a life at all.

Love Stories

Harry Potter is one of the latest mythological superstars in the world, but he certainly isn't the first. When I was a kid, E.T. could have gotten elected. Moviegoers for the last couple of decades have enjoyed movies about various mythological men, men who are part bat, part spider, and all super.

Myths seem a lot like love to me. They aren't measurable or rational, yet they make life make sense when we let go of our rational world and experience them. Especially when we are children, we seem to chase myths like adults chase love. We chase myths as if we intrinsically know that life without something grand and mystical isn't really life at all.

These moments when we get to sit in a theater are really just moments to stand outside of ourselves and awaken our imaginations to the hope that life isn't just a series of moments or a scientific coincidence.

As Gary Laderman stated, film gives us "an escape from reality and effective interpretive tools to make sense of reality."[1] As we sit in a theater and watch these stories play out, we are entering into an entertaining but a deeply religious experience. These mythological stories tell us that good ultimately is better than evil, love is better than hate, and even characters that seem insignificant can have significance.

Filmmakers have become the new prophets who tell us what direction our lives should take. These films and novels pick up where the Scriptures leave off in our lives; they become an authoritative script over us. It happens subtly. It can even happen while we are attending a church. This is why churches are filled with those of us who can quote hundreds of lines from our favorite film and zero Old Testament poetry. If we even know there is Old Testament poetry. In the same way as love, these myths create meaning to why we exist in the world.

In Need of a Myth

For as long as I can remember, I have been in school. From preschool to high school to grad school, there has always been something to study. Consequently, I have never really understood reading something or watching something that I knew wasn't true. I have always preferred facts to myth.

In many ways our education has kept us limited to focusing our lives on what we can know and see, not on what is outside the bounds of our wildest dreams. It is this kind of culture that needs Harry Potter and Superman. All of these superhero movies have something in common: they allow us to be less rational and reasonable, and they invite the imagination into our life experience. We are hungry for these myths; they give us pictures of something a little less tame than our world, and they allow us to safely follow our intuition that there is more to life than we can see.

We are now entering an age where the truth in many ways is being trumped by myth; science is being replaced by mystery. At the turn of the twentieth century, our world was curious about what it could know. At the turn of the twenty-first century, our world is more curious about what it cannot know.[2]

Superhero Jesus

The fiercest critics of the Christian faith in our culture accuse it of being a myth. As a reaction to this, often Christianity has spent its energy on proving why it is a viable option for people on a religious quest. If we haven't focused on proving why Jesus really got up from the dead, we have focused on rationalizing salvation or giving ourselves more practical principles that should shape the way we live our lives. But maybe being accused of being a myth isn't that bad.

As Christianity has reduced itself to absolute truths and reasoned faith to combat the fear of being labeled a myth, we have to ask, Isn't Christianity a myth? I am not talking about in the fictional sense, but in the sense of what it is telling us in its own Scriptures. Fully human, fully divine—this man descended upon our earth, he was beloved by children, and he had the power to heal. He was hated by the authorities; and against the cries of those who loved him, the authorities captured him and killed him. Only death couldn't hold him, and he went back to where he came from.

Who am I talking about? Jesus or E.T.? All of the great myths and stories of our age that fascinate children with tales of magic and conquering death, all borrow from the story of Jesus. Even the greatest movies can be traced back in some way to be found in the greatest myth of all time. We all want these stories to be true, and we find in the Scriptures that what we long for *is* true. It is the greatest story ever told, filled with angels, demons, death, and redemption.

If this is true, then why is the gospel that we come to know as small children so empty of grand narrative? To live out our Christian faith without delving into the mythological side is like living life without chasing love. Nothing about following Jesus can make sense until we surrender to mystery.

I think most of us want our Christian faith to exist without the faith—I know I do. But until you let go and throw yourself into the hope of how grand the story actually is—like the moment you let go of yourself long enough to fall in love with someone, resting your life on a hope that they are actually who you want them to be—it doesn't make sense. The beautiful and troubling paradox of the Christian faith is that it has to be a faith, not a proven formula.

Every once in a while as Christians, we see hints of another world here; we feel like we are part of something bigger than just the Earth itself, but the moments seem so seldom that we treat them more like a rumor we hear than a reality we are living in. Occasionally when I am flipping through the channels on television, I will stop and watch the Christian network when they have one of those faith healers on. I have never known what to think about them. I only have been trained to think that if it is not rational and tame, it is not Jesus. But these guys fascinate me.

They perform miracles and they talk in foreign languages, almost as if they are not human. Part of me wonders if I am not as good of a Christian because I can't heal anyone. Part of me wonders if I could heal someone, but I have never tried. In the end, I always change the channel and return to a much more tame faith and way of relating to Jesus.

Thomas Jefferson, the third president of the United States, had a Bible but hardly called himself a Christian. He kept a Bible in which he cut out all of the things that didn't make sense. If it were a miracle, he would cut it out. If it were a story about God speaking to man, he would cut it out. In the end, he was left with just some good teachings and practical insights.

On the face of it, any Christian would say this is pure sacrilege. But is it really that different from how we believe the Bible? We have eliminated or played down the parts that don't make sense to us, and we have taken away the myth before our very eyes. We have made it all profoundly civil. If God wanted us to read the Bible for just practical insight, why did he put all the other stuff in there? Why is it so filled with glorious tales that seem ripped out of a Harry Potter novel? Where the practical teachings are valid in their own way, the myth of the Bible invites us into it, and everyone has a role to play.

Your Kingdom Come

The Bible is filled with words that we don't use anymore, words that seem passed down from a time that hasn't existed in centuries. One of those words is *kingdom*. The only kingdom I know anything about is the United Kingdom, and while I love Austin Powers and believe Elton John's "Tiny Dancer" is one of the greatest songs in Billboard history, I don't think they are what Jesus had in mind. Most church services I've been to mention God's kingdom at some point, but no one ever seems able to explain it in terms that are comprehensible.

Maybe the kingdom is like love, and I'm so busy looking for a way to measure it that I am incapable of experiencing it. I suppose I haven't bothered to research it much, and I always assumed "God's kingdom" and "heaven" were the same ideas. Because we think of heaven as some place we are all going to when we die, I never thought of God's kingdom as having implications for life on this earth. But when you read the Bible, especially the life of Jesus, you have to begin to ask questions about a coming kingdom; you have to visit the other "romantic" side of faith. And when you do, you all the sudden begin to understand we are being invited into a great myth, a myth far greater than the Harry Potter myth. A myth far greater than our churches and Bible studies would lead us to believe.

When Jesus invited his followers to pray, he told them to pray, God's Kingdom come, His will be done, on Earth as it is in Heaven.[3] What does this mean? This sounds more like the language of the faith healers and miracle workers on TV than what I am used to. Throughout the gospels of Matthew, Mark, and Luke, it is repeatedly announced, the Kingdom of God is at hand.[4] Is this just religious language and metaphor, or is there an actual kingdom that we are now living in, a kingdom that has come to Earth and has literal power? Why then do we never seem to understand this message of Jesus about his kingdom?

So what is God's kingdom, what is this "kingdom at hand"? To understand this grand myth takes more imagination than reason, more heart than mind.

At the time of Jesus, the world was ruled by the Roman Empire, and this man named Caesar ruled the Roman Empire. The Roman Empire was a brutal regime, and the Caesars were just as brutal. To give you a sense of it, there's this "triumphal arch" in the Roman forum—the "old Rome" that was the center of Caesar's empire. During one conquest where they conquered Israel, they marched prisoners back and made them build this arch. That would be punishment enough, except that the entire arch was laden with the story of their defeat. Some Israelite thousands of years ago had to place and mortar an artfully carved stone depicting the destruction of a menorah and the Ark of the Covenant being carried away by conquerors. This was their psychological warfare.

But in taking over the world, the Romans were engaged in gruesome physical warfare, too, and they would use any means necessary. The cross was Rome's great invention of fear because of the untold pain it caused its victims. The cross wasn't a religious metaphor, as we understand it today; it wasn't something in gold around someone's neck; it was the worst killing device anyone had ever invented. It was also a symbol of Rome's power throughout the world. Long before Jesus, anyone who subverted this kingdom would be murdered on a cross.

The nation of Israel, where Jesus was born, was under the reign of the Roman Empire.[5] Jesus himself would have to bow to Caesar's decrees. The nation of Israel had a dilemma; they believed their God was sovereign, yet on Earth, Caesar was sovereign. He even taught people that he was god.

So Israel at this time was a marginalized group of people in the corner of Rome's empire. They had to give all of their money to Rome, and they were beginning to starve to death while Rome got richer. People were oppressed and needy, and they were losing their identity along with their power. This is the world that Jesus stepped into.

Caesar was building a kingdom. It was about murder, injustice, vanity, and power. Jesus came on the scene and began to invite people into another kingdom, a subversive kingdom. It was a totally different kind of kingdom. It wasn't about murder and injustice; it was about love and forgiveness. To use the word *kingdom* at this time in reference to anything other than Caesar would have gotten you killed. It was even worse to say that you were God and Caesar wasn't. But this was Jesus' message. Essentially Jesus was saying Caesar is going down. His rule is over. There is a new sheriff in town.

This message began to spread because among the oppressed it was much needed. And it was working. Jesus was getting tax collectors to follow him instead of Caesar, meaning Caesar and his people were losing money. All of a sudden the kingdom of Jesus was having political, social, and economic implications.

So where one kingdom was visible with murder and buildings, the other was invisible and intangible. It had a mythic power built on ideas like justice, redemption, and a genuine encounter with the divine Creator of the universe.

Jesus then began to teach that his kingdom was ultimately going to win. No one in Caesar's kingdom liked this, and this is why Jesus was hunted down and murdered. At the cross his kingdom had seemingly come to an end. When you read the story of Jesus through this lens, you are all of the sudden a hundred pages into a novel that you can't put down. This real-life myth is filled with twists and turns, and the fate of the world is left hanging in the balance when the main character is left hanging on a cross.

Your Will Be Done

I have often wondered why the cross was necessary. I trust and know that God is in control, but why did it have to happen in such a brutal fashion? Couldn't he have let his son off a little easier? The brutality of the cross comes into focus with the lens of the kingdom. The cross was the symbol of Rome's kingdom. It represented death, which was the last thing Jesus had to defeat for his message to win. With the cross, Jesus changed the scope and law of the universe. He took the best shot of the Caesar.

He was bloodied, spit on, stripped naked in public, and

murdered. It was impossible for anything worse to happen. And who did it? The Roman soldiers. Essentially those who believed that Caesar, not Jesus, was their god. What is amazing about the story of the cross is that throughout the torture, Jesus always responds with love. Even hanging on the cross, he invites forgiveness for his enemies. Right until the bloody end, Jesus is teaching how his kingdom works. He is teaching, even as he is dying, that his kingdom has come. Who watching in that moment would have seen Jesus as a king? Who would have watched him and thought he had won? You had to look deeper.

His message wasn't about winning in the world's eyes. His message was upside down. He had to show that his kingdom was the complete opposite of Caesar's. His kingdom wasn't about murdering the crowd for the glory of the king. His kingdom was about the king being murdered and giving life to the crowd. When Jesus rose from the dead, he didn't just say that he defeated death; he said that he had overcome the world. He had overcome the kingdoms of injustice and violence, persecution and murder; and by defeating the cross, he defeated all powers that were unjust and ruled the world.[6]

The cross was necessary for Jesus to submit to the evil powers so that he could defeat them.[7] To overcome evil, he had to go through it. When he left the world, he left his kingdom. And he handed it off to his followers to advance.

We are now the agents of the kingdom. Jesus has cleared

the path and given us the keys to build the kingdom here on this earth—the authority he has is now ours. The writers of the New Testament believed this to be reality. They believed this to be their message and mission. Power and authority was theirs, but not in the traditional sense. Not in buildings and earthly kingdoms—in hearts and souls. It is still an upside down, invisible kingdom.

Perhaps what is most chilling to me is that eventually Jesus' kingdom did win. In the 300s, the Roman emperor, Constantine, became a follower of Jesus. Think about the implications of that. Jesus, in time, overcame the evil and power that murdered him, and they were now in his kingdom. In AD 337, crosses were banned. I get weepy when I think about Jesus being murdered on a cross. But I get a knot in my throat when I realize that the very people who murdered him on it, because they now were bowing to him, banned the cross, the thing Jesus was murdered on. Their reign of terror was over. Jesus' reign was just getting started. This is greater than any Harry Potter novel. This is better than *Lord of the Rings*. This myth is reality. And when we follow Jesus, we are in it and a part of it.

So to follow Jesus, we don't just follow him; we submit to his kingdom of love and grace. We now believe that this is the prevailing force in the world. Our God has literally overcome the world. Love has won. When I look at the world today, I see a world that is desperately in need of the kingdom of Jesus. There are lots of Caesars in our day. And seemingly they often win.

The abandonment you have experienced is perhaps your Caesar. For the kid who watched his parents split, for the girl who is the victim of abuse, our culture is crying out to know that injustice and hatred don't win. We need to know that we are a part of a grand story, a great myth, and that in the end of our story, love and mercy will prevail. Every crooked path will be made straight, even when it seems impossible.

We often choose just to sit in church services that teach us to be good people, to serve, and to be nice to one another. But perhaps we forget to mention that the world has been over-come, and the things that seem unfair here now are going to be made right in their time. As a follower of Jesus, I don't just put my faith in him; I also have to put my faith in his kingdom. To believe that I am just supposed to go to heaven if I believe the right things is an illusion. To believe that the kingdom of God is only in heaven is an illusion. The kingdom is here, and it becomes true the moment we realize the mes-sage of Christianity is far greater than we had hoped. This kingdom hasn't just come. It is coming.

On Earth as It Is in Heaven

We do not live in a time when the kingdom of God is fully realized; we live in a time when it is still growing and advancing, awaiting the return of its King to right all wrongs. This myth that we are a part of is still ongoing. But as followers of Jesus, we have a role to play in this myth. We are the agents who believe we have power over all the kingdoms of this world, and we have the ability to advance the kingdom of God anywhere.

To follow Jesus means we believe in a mythological reality. It means we submit to it. In a world that seeks vanity and power first, we believe those things will diminish and disappear. To live this out, it means we always believe that love is a better option than hate and that grace is better toward our enemies than hatred. The cross has defeated these powers of evil that are present in our world, and we can build the kingdom of Jesus right on their backs. When we do, we bring heaven to Earth. Love will always defeat evil. Hate will always lose. The kingdom has come. And it is still coming.

ELEVEN

THE DESTINATION OF RENOVATION

GOING BACK TO GO FORWARD

When I was in college, I helped lead a mission trip with a group of high school students to Eastern Europe. I've always struggled with short-term mission trips, especially ones to an exotic location. It always leaves me feeling more like a Christian tourist than it does a missionary. On this particular trip, we stopped over in Vienna, Austria, for a few days. While the rest of the trip was filled with moments of serving, our purpose in Vienna was seeing.

There was something profound about being in a place that was so old. Every corner you turned had a different relic, a plaque marking hundreds of years of history. Vienna is older than the Christian faith itself and has a skyline shaped by imperial palaces from a world that doesn't exist anymore. They have churches that seem as old as faith itself and a zoo that is older than America. Even the food they serve tastes like tradition. For those of us from the States, there is a magical nature to places in the world that have so much history. I was raised in a town where the oldest architecture I can recall is a Wal-Mart.

We live in a world where we appreciate something that is vintage. In fact, being aged adds to its aesthetic; it doesn't take away. Perhaps you are drawn to architecture that feels old or to clothing that is preworn. We pay hundreds of dollars more for a pair of jeans that comes destroyed, thousands more for furniture with that vintage feel, and tens of thousands on homes with a historic look.

This is an interesting twinge about us; we are constantly reaching for something new, an innovative gadget, while never forgetting to connect to something old. We want this feel in our clothes and homes; we want to know that we are connected to history. Hence the popularity of Chuck Taylor shoes and the timeless sound of Frank Sinatra.

In the process of pursuing a new way of understanding our faith, we cannot forsake our history. We belong to an ancient tradition, the sons and daughters of sons and daughters who built their lives on the message of Jesus. If we are not careful, we can tear down the old. In the process, we can forsake the voices of mentors, leaders, churches, and thinkers who remind us that we are a part of something that expands beyond our lifetime. Christian spirituality has the beauty of Vienna.

This Old House

My dad owned a construction business when I was a kid, something he did to supplement his pastor's salary, and he would occasionally book jobs in the historic district of town. He would often take me with him, and he would be asked to repair or add to something that had existed for seventy years or so. My dad would fix and repair, rebuild and restore, always trying to match his craftsmanship to the vision of the original builder. He always understood that you don't stick a 1990s-style porch on a 1900s-style house. You begin the work with the belief that there is something good there, and it is worth preserving. My job in these situations was part education and part entertainment. My dad would show me how to patch a leaky roof, and I would make him laugh by telling him the house smelled like soup. These were some of the best moments I recall with my dad, where we did something together and he taught me the difference between demolition and renovation.

As we approach the Christian faith, no matter how wounded we have been by a particular version of it, I hope we understand the difference between these two. We are called to renovate, not demolish. We approach our faith like an old house; we start with the assumption that a lot is good and must be kept. We keep in mind the vision of the original architect.

The first reason we must renovate and not demolish is to stay connected to something old. I have served on staff at two large and modern churches and had a wonderful experience and relationship with both. I still attend those churches sometimes and have great experiences there to this day, but they can feel like a stroll through a mall or supermarket. My wife and I recently discovered a little Episcopal church close to our house that we occasionally go to. When you step into the sanctuary, it is filled with icons of the church, liturgy that has been spoken for hundreds of years, and wonderful songs being sung in a language I don't speak.

While it can be a foreign experience, walking into the building reminds me that I am connected to something old. Sometimes I need to go to church in Vienna, not Wal-Mart. It is possible your church experience could be described with lots of adjectives, from entertaining to boring—but would you say *ancient*? Did it tell you where you belong in history? Did it show you what to be a part of? Even if some of it seemed too ancient, we all long for that sense that we belong to something from a different time and place. When it comes to church, as Ray Anderson stated, "A venerable history is more compelling than a vulnerable future."[1]

If you are like me, you have memories of asking your grandparents stories of where they came from and what made them who they are. In many ways, this tells you who you are. Abandonment has left us without a sense of history, and not knowing where we came from can paralyze us from knowing where we are going. The beauty of the Christian story is that it is an ancient story, telling a story of the world and where it is going. While you may not long for your old church experience, you do long to be connected to something older and bigger than yourself. We have all been raised in a scientific and sterile environment, made to explain and reduce things down to function and rationality. When we enter a building that isn't about either of those, it is good for the soul.

Another reason we must have a commitment to renovation and not demolition is that there are profound lessons to learn from history. When I write this book and you read it, we must recognize we are in a long line of thinkers. Our story is not new. You are one of many to feel what you feel. Being frustrated with the church is as deep in Christian history as Jesus himself. When we forget this, we feel as though we are special victims, somehow justified in our rage, validated in our anger. We must remember that, as David Dark stated, "deeply sincere people have gone to houses of worship, looked after their families, and prayed intensely while also participating in unthinkable atrocities."[2] Our faith story is connected to a long and broken mess of God's people.

History teaches us that we are people of the pendulum, reacting strongly when problems arise. If there is a lesson for us, it is that we shouldn't demolish what we have but renovate instead. Perhaps you push strongly against the legalism of your parents' faith, and you traded legalism for license some time ago. The Old and the New Testaments stand together to show that God invites the tension between those two, and we shouldn't swing to one or the other. I hope we won't swing too far, that we'd remember the middle ground is the higher ground.

You may want to start new, tempted to chunk the foundations that you built your life on, but you don't need something new, you need something old. As you contemplate your spiritual journey, be careful that your actions aren't reactions, looking for something that wasn't allowed. Our parents were people of the pendulum, and now we are reacting to their swing in our generation. If we react back, this will be as empty as the place you started.

Our doubt, disillusionment, and dissatisfaction eventually come full circle, and we realize the faith we abandoned was our best hope at making sense of our world. I hope your story is different. I hope your story does the harder work of renovation. It's more difficult to decide that a system or a church has jaded you deeply but that you are committed to it. As you continually weigh your spiritual journey in a popular culture that is a church, there will no doubt be options for you to turn to, giving you a different narrative of the world than the one you heard in your childhood, different gods that vie for your allegiance, even if they aren't wearing a religious mask.

As we are inundated with a constant stream of voices, may we remember that while the church is broken, it is coherent in its explanation of what it means to be in the world. The gift of the Christian faith and its beauty is that it gives us an overarching story that we exist in. When I meet people who leave the Christian faith, no matter what made them leave, they never seem to find another coherent story.[3] More times than not, a demolition leads to a fragmentation, a fragmentation that drives them deeper into a pit of wandering.

While our culture is filled with spirituality, it isn't filled with spiritual coherence. We are called on to give, to be moral, to be happy, all while being transcendental, but for what purpose? Is it so we feel good? What is the end goal? Usually there isn't one. At the same time, we are encouraged to be consumers, to do what we want, when we want; life filled without even a hint of spirituality.

Our culture is calling us to ride two horses that are going different directions, with the catastrophic result of fragmentation. This forces us deeper into the predicament of wandering the world, asking, Who are we? Why are we here? Where do we belong? Perhaps this is your story. You realize you demolished your Christian faith, but when you exited that story you found yourself in a different one without realizing it. You may be riding a different horse (or several), but where are you going?

When we choose the process of renovation, infusing

something ancient into something new, we are offered a way out of fragmentation; we are offered coherence—one horse, taking one path. Our lives take place in a spiritual maze, without a framework or an ending point. The story of a God who created the world, a Son who redeemed it, and a God who will ultimately restore it, gives us a way to make sense of it. Renovation strips us to the basics of the Christian faith, no matter what your rub has been with religion. If you have renounced the faith, did you renounce the narrative?

With the fishbowl shattered and the renovation beginning, we cling to the basics. Some of us were badly wounded because these basics were forgotten. Perhaps you were taught a series of biblical opinions, about what to drink and watch, where to go, and even who to be around, but you weren't given any biblical convictions. The framework, the foundation of the entire story, is about a God who created it, saved it, will restore it—and who invites us into it. We can go a thousand directions from there, and we do, but may we begin with the beautiful foundation as we renovate. If your church experience felt a little like someone built the house for you and told you what to put into it, how to decorate, and how long the curtains need to be, what was the frustrating part? Looking back, do you appreciate the foundation? Wasn't what forced you away was when they told you exactly how the house should look?

We don't need all of the opinions—we can and will draw our own. We do need this beautiful, bedrock foundation. We can decide from there what we want it to look like. As Paul wrote in Philippians 2:12, we can work it out with fear and trembling. If not, we will perhaps choose to knock the whole house down, having nowhere to live at all, no story to call home.

Renovation is a path of coherence. You and I need that. We have wanted it since we entered this world. Whether we end up lost or found hangs in the balance with what we decide to do.

May we take with us something core on our spiritual path. May we be people who explore something new, while we are anchored in something really old.

ACKNOWLEDGMENTS

To Bryan Norman—you and Suzanne are beautiful people. You made this project happen. Thank you.

To Don Jacobson—your family and mentorship mean the world to me. Thank you.

Lanny Donoho—you entrusted me with a lot when I had done very little. Thank you.

Kevin Ragsdale—you told me I could do this when I didn't even know what I was doing. Thank you.

Reggie Joiner—you are the most loyal and generous person I know. Thank you.

XP3 Team—I never thought I could love a job this much. Thank you.

Mom and Dad—you taught me what faith is. I'm still holding on. Thank you.

Special thanks to the movie *Fight Club*. I watched it several times throughout the original writing of this book. Special thanks to Ray Lamontagne; you were singing to me throughout lots of rewrites. Also, the music of Brett Dennen, Blind Pilot, Pedro the Lion (David Bazan's "Lost My Shape" was listened to on repeat throughout the writing of Chapter 4), Gary Allan, Jamey Johnson, Patty Griffin's *Downtown Church* album, Raymond Miles' *A Taste of Heaven* album, U2, David Nail's *I'm About to Come Alive*, Allison Krauss, Keith Urban, the Charlie Hall Band, and, of course, Garth Brooks.

I am also greatly indebted to many authors and teachers along the way who have helped me. In many ways, I stand on their shoulders. This book wouldn't have been written had it not been for my time at Fuller Seminary and the tons of lectures and books I heard and read. Barry Taylor and Chap Clark in particular are tour guides for me in this spiritual conversation. Chap Clark's book, *Hurt*, provides so much of the sociological lens that is used in this book. Barry Taylor and Craig Detweiler's book, *Matrix of Meanings*, provides so much of the theological lens that is used.

I lost my faith in their classrooms—and found one I like much better.

NOTES

Prologue

1. Fascinating thinker about the place of Christianity in the world. Christopher Partridge, *Re-Enchantment of the West: Volume 1 Alternative Spiritualities, Sacralization, Popular Culture and Occulture* (New York: T & T Clark International, 2005).

Chapter 1

1. Dr. Chap Clark has done extensive research and lectures on the landscape of adolescence. For further education, I would highly recommend reading his book *Hurt: Inside the world of Today's Teenagers* (Grand Rapids: Baker Academic, 2004). I explored these ideas in his class, Foundations of Youth Ministry, in the fall of 2004, at Fuller Theological Seminary.
2. G. Stanley Hall coined the word *adolescence* in 1904 in *Adolescence: Its Psychology and Its Relations to Physiology, Anthropology, Sociology, Sex, Crime, Religion and Education* (Ithaca, NY: Cornell University Library, 2009).
3. Barry Taylor was a teacher of mine at Fuller Theological Seminary. He was a sound engineer for AC/DC, and I think he even became a Christian on the "Highway to Hell"

tour. For that reason alone, read everything he writes. He is now the Rev. Rockstar emeritus in Pasadena, and his work has been crucial for me. In his introductory portion of *Entertainment Theology*, he talks about the mixture of voices in our lives. Barry Taylor, *Entertainment Theology: New-Edge Spirituality in a Digital Democracy* (Grand Rapids: Baker Academic, 2008), 17.

4. Craig Detweiler and Barry Taylor, *A Matrix of Meanings: Finding God in Pop Culture* (Grand Rapids: Baker Academic, 2003), 296.

5. Erwin McManus, a prominent pastor at Mosaic Church, Los Angeles, has spoken and written on this idea. For more, read *Uprising: A Revolution of the Soul* (Nashville: Thomas Nelson, 2003), 134.

Chapter 2

1. From Barry Taylor's karma lecture in his Postmodern Theology course, fall 2005, Fuller Theological Seminary, Pasadena, California. In Barry Taylor's fall 2005 class, this topic was explored in lecture and discussion with classmates. It was the first time I began to think about Christianity for the next generation.

2. Rob Bell, *Velvet Elvis: Repainting the Christian Faith* (Grand Rapids: Zondervan, 2005). Rob Bell explores this idea in *Velvet Elvis*. He actually makes the point that *Christian* is better as a noun than as an adjective.

3. Galatians 2:11 NIV.

Chapter 3

1. Rob Bell explores this idea in his sermon "Theology of the Clicks" (www.marshill.org).

Chapter 4

1. Pat Conroy, *Beach Music* (New York: Doubleday, 1995), 6. Pat Conroy is one of my favorite authors, and a staple for a Southern gentleman.
2. Mother Teresa and Brian Kolodiejchuk, *Mother Teresa: Come Be My Light* (New York: Doubleday, 2007), 169, 189, 193.

Chapter 5

1. Tom Beaudoin, *Virtual Faith: The Irreverent Spiritual Quest of Generation X* (Jossey-Bass, 1998). Tom Beaudoin has written extensively on the place of the Christian faith in our culture.
2. I heard Erwin McManus reference this from a *USA Today* article, while attending a Catalyst Conference in Duluth, Georgia, in the fall of 2003.
3. My dear friend Lanny Donoho has done profound work in Kenya. He provided me with this insight. His organization 410 Bridge is working hard to insert the word *future* into the Swahili language. He and I had this conversation on a bus in Santa Cruz, Bolivia, in May 2005.
4. John Eldridge, *Wild at Heart* (Nashville: Thomas Nelson, 2001). I discovered John Eldridge's work, *Wild at Heart*, in the fall of 2001. This book was the first time I discovered I needed my heart connected to the rest of my life. Brilliant book.
5. G. K. Chesterton, *Orthodoxy* (Chicago: Moody Publishers, 2009), 26–49. Gilbert Keith Chesterton's quote is loaded, and if you are like me, it will take you a lifetime to get your head around it. This quote comes from the chapter titled "The Maniac."

Chapter 6

1. Rock Harbor Church in Costa Mesa, California, is the only place I know of where thousands of college students show up to worship God in Southern California. I had the privilege of

being a teaching pastor there when I lived in Orange County. Awesome place. I met my wife there too.

2. Detweiler and Taylor, *A Matrix of Meanings*, 243–269. Detweiler and Taylor explore the downswing of the institution of sports.

3. I included a U2 reference because a Christian book with any edge to it has to include a U2 reference.

4. Greg Boyd explores this topic in his book, *The Myth of a Christian Nation*. Gregory A. Boyd, *The Myth of a Christian Nation: How the Quest for Political Power Is Destroying the Church* (Grand Rapids: Zondervan, 2007).

5. Walter Brueggemann, *Mandate to Difference: An Invitation to the Contemporary Church* (Louisville: Westminster John Knox Press, 2007), 203. Walter Brueggemann is one of the most respected theologians to ever live. Coincidentally, he lived next door to my grandfather when I was a kid, and I would often see him outside, and I even went in his house one time and talked with him. In seminary, many classes were assigned his books, and it took me a while to figure out I knew him. A few years ago Rosanna and I did a house church for a year focusing on his book.

6. The "exodus to exile" concept comes from a lecture given by Alan Roxburgh on November 13, 2002, at Fuller Theological Seminary.

Chapter 7

1. Peter Rollins, *The Orthodox Heretic: And Other Impossible Tales* (Orleans, MA: Paraclete Press, 2009), 39.

2. I heard Randall Wallace say this at the City of Angels Film Festival, October 2006.

Chapter 8

1. James B. Nelson, *Body Theology* (Louisville, KY: Westminster John Knox Press, 1992). James Nelson's work on "body

theology" helped me immensely. This section is referring to his section, "Starting with Experience" in chapter 3.

2. Taylor and Detweiler say, "In a post-human society, body modification identifies flesh as the last 'permanent' possession." This section is interacting with that idea and a doctoral project they did. Detweiler and Taylor, *A Matrix of Meanings* (Grand Rapids: Baker Academic, 2003), 234.

3. Tom Beaudoin's thoughts about tattoos and the body were in my mind as I wrote this. Tom Beaudoin, *Virtual Faith: The Irreverent Spiritual Quest of Generation X* (Jossey-Bass, 1998).

4. "We do not just have bodies, we are bodies." James B. Nelson, *Body Theology*, 43.

5. This end section was inspired by my reading of *A Hidden Wholeness*. This is one of those books that you will be glad you read—but the people around you will be eternally grateful you read it. Parker J. Palmer, *A Hidden Wholeness: The Journey Toward an Undivided Life* (Jossey-Bass, 2009).

Chapter 9

1. Neil Postman, *Technopoly: The Surrender of Technology to Culture* (New York: Vintage, 1993), 26. Neil Postman's work *Technopoly* is a must read. His thoughts shaped my perspective for this entire chapter. He uses da Vinci as an illustration.

2. Ibid.

3. *The Technological Society* by Jacques Tellul is also worth exploring but is a tougher read than Postman. Tellul helped shape my thoughts in this chapter. Tellul was way ahead of his time—amazing that a Frenchman in 1964 was able to predict twenty-first-century American culture. Jacques Tellul, *The Technological Society* (New York: Vintage, 1967).

4. Postman, *Technopoly* (New York: Vintage, 1993), 54.

5. This is another Postman reference, from his book about the effects of television. *Amusing Ourselves to Death: Public Discourse in the Age of Show Business* (New York: Penguin, 2005).

6. "The most interesting conclusion we came to is that

millennials don't talk about cars the way previous generations did. It used to be that when you turned 16 you went down to the DMV and got your license, but young people care more about their cell phones then they do their cars." Part of the reason for this is that young people use Facebook, Twitter, and IM to stay in touch, so physical proximity doesn't matter as much as it used to. Mike Cooperman, J. D. Power & Associates survey, industrybnet.com, February 22, 2010.

7. Erik Davis calls technology a "trickster." He says it is making promises it doesn't keep. Like this false connection. His book *TechGnosis* is a brilliant book. Erik Davis, *TechGnosis: Myth, Magic & Mysticism in the Age of Information* (Waterville, Maine: Five Star, 2005).

8. My dear friend and fellow writer, Abbi Sprunger, e-mailed this to me in private correspondence in the fall of 2006. I was speaking at a conference that she was involved with, and she was e-mailing all the speakers to tell them she was praying for them. I don't know how she knew to pray for this for me, but I have never forgotten, and I desperately needed to hear it.

9. This story is told in Mark 5:1–20.

Chapter 10

1. Gary Laderman, *Sacred Matters: Celebrity Worship, Sexual Ecstasies, the Living Dead, and Other Signs of Religious Life in the United States* (New York: The New Press, 2010), 10.

2. The following sentence inspired this thought. "Thanks to science, it has been said, the twentieth century began in certainty and ended in uncertainty." Spencer Burke and Barry Taylor, *A Heretic's Guide to Eternity* (Jossey-Bass, 2006), xviii.

3. From Matthew 6:10 NIV.

4. My introduction to Jesus' message of the kingdom came courtesy of George Eldon Ladd. G. E. Ladd, *A Theology of the New Testament* (Grand Rapids: Eerdmans, 1993).

5. There are lots of good resources for understanding the Roman Empire's interaction with Jesus. I like this one.

Richard A. Horsley, *Jesus and Empire: The Kingdom of God and the New World Disorder* (Philadelphia: Fortress Press, 2003).
6. Rob Bell gives a beautiful account of the cross in a sermon he gives, "Love Wins" (http://marshill.org/rob-bell/love-wins/).
7. John Howard Yoder, *The Politics of Jesus* (Grand Rapids: Eerdmans, 1994). Yoder calls this act of submission "revolutionary subordination." His understanding of the cross leads him to nonviolence.

Chapter 11

1. Ray Anderson, *An Emergent Theology for Emerging Churches* (Downers Grove, IL: IVP, 2006), 200–1.
2. David Dark, *The Sacredness of Questioning Everything* (Grand Rapids: Zondervan, 2009), 173.
3. The idea of "coherence" comes from Jonathan Wilson's *Living Faithfully in a Fragmented World*. Jonathan Wilson, *Living Faithfully in a Fragmented World: Lessons for the Church from Macintyre's After Virtue* (Eugene, OR: Wipf and Stock, 2008), 40.

DISCUSSION
QUESTIONS

Chapter 1

1. Think about your worldview. Is your first response to question or defend it?
2. Walter Brueggemann said, "Interpretation is an inescapable human activity." Think about the church, people, and environment through which Jesus came to you. Whoever and wherever it was, they interpreted it through their life experiences and worldview. Did anything get lost when they translated it to you?

3. Just like those before us, we interpret Jesus through our experiences. How has abandonment shaped your faith?

4. How would you define the difference between Jesus and the church?

5. If abandonment is shaping a generation, is Jesus irrelevant or more relevant than ever?

Chapter 2

1. How would you define spirituality?

2. Why is being spiritual so much more attractive than being a Christian in our culture?

3. In your experience, is being a Christian a spiritual activity?

4. What is something you do (work, music, sports, film, etc.) that would perhaps be defined as "secular" but to you is "sacred"?

5. Christianity is about leaving an illusion for a reality. What is an illusion you find yourself trapped in? What would a step toward reality be?

Chapter 3

1. Do you tend to be more of a drip artist or a sketch artist?

2. Guilt doesn't come from God. It comes from learning the wrong way to paint. Perhaps you or someone you know has walked away from the Christian faith. Was the issue Jesus, or was the issue being a sketch artist?

3. Cornel West said in reference to economics, "Being born on 3rd base doesn't mean you hit a triple." I think the same is true spiritually. What base were you born on?

4. Do you feel like you have a long way to go or only a short distance?

5. Do you celebrate the steps people take, or do you point out the ones they don't? Do you celebrate the steps you take, or do you just think about the ones you haven't taken yet?

Chapter 4

1. Martin Luther said, "Only God and certain madmen have no doubts." Has there ever been a time in your faith where you had doubt but felt like you couldn't talk about it?

2. How are doubt and faith similar? How are they different?

3. As you get older, does it seem easier to get disillusioned? Why?

4. In my life I have noticed that when disillusionment goes unattended it turns into disengagement. Is disengagement *from* God a result of disillusionment *with* God?

5. Are you more afraid of being miserable, or of mystery?

Chapter 5

1. Who are some of your favorite musicians? If the divide between the sacred and secular is a false one, then what songs and what lines have led you closer to God and reality?

2. What does the gift of music to humanity say about God's character?

3. Describe a moment where your heart and mind have been in different places.

4. Do you tend to trust your heart, or to be skeptical of it?

5. Why does following Jesus have to be an act of the heart, not just a mental exercise?

Chapter 6

1. If you had the option of the mall or the anti-mall, which one would you go to?

2. How do you turn skepticism of politics and institutions into engagement with them? Where is

the balance for you? Do you find it important to vote? Why or why not?

3. If a "culture war" is the wrong fight, then what is the right way to fight for and stand for something you are convinced is right?

4. There used to be a bumper sticker that said, "Think Globally, Act Locally." While it is important to think globally about the position of the church, how do you locally live out a faith that is faithful to the "ideas" of Jesus, before the "institution" of the church?

5. In your everyday life, what is a practical way to carry faith "in exile"? Do you think that applies to all religion in a globalized world, or just to Christianity?

Chapter 7

1. How has pain shaped your view of God, yourself, and the world?

2. While there is no right or wrong answer to how a person deals with pain, do you tend to give a simple answer to question number 1, or a complex one? (For example, do you say something like, "Pain can make you bitter or better, and I got better." Or do you tend to say, "It's a long story, and I still don't know the answer.")

3. Have Christians been helpful or hurtful in dealing with your pain?

4. What are some films (give specific lines or scenes) that have helped you deal with tragedy?

5. What is the balance between hope and reality?

Chapter 8

1. How did your parents, church, or culture raise you to think about your body?

2. Is your view of the body "embodied" like Pasadena, or "dualistic" like Atlanta?

3. How does a "dualistic" approach keep someone distant from God? How does sexuality (or sexual struggles), suffer or benefit from dualism?

4. How would you describe your avatar (fashion, tattoos, etc.)? How did that come about for you? What does that say about your spirituality? Has your faith background made you feel guilty about your avatar, has it celebrated it, or has it seemed irrelevant?

5. What is something about your body that you really like?

Chapter 9

1. How would you define your relationship to technology? Are you ever skeptical of its effects, or do you inconspicuously consume?
2. If we let it, technology makes us efficient and uninteresting. In what ways do you engage with life (dancing, music, learning a language, etc.) to be interesting beyond some sort of device?
3. Do you have "meaningful silence" built into your life?
4. If you are honest, is being loved or being admired of more wealth to you?
5. What is something about life one hundred years ago you would have really enjoyed?

Chapter 10

1. What is your favorite myth, currently and from childhood? Why that one over others?
2. As a kid, how did you become that character? Did you dress up like him or her for Halloween? What did that say about how you once perceived the world?
3. How are faith and belief different?
4. To enter into a Christian faith, we also enter into the grandness of the kingdom of God. Why do you think God chose a kingdom as a metaphor?

5. With no divide between the sacred and the secular, where would you say God's kingdom is at work in your life?

Chapter 11

1. Think about purchases you recently have made. Do you prefer things that are vintage or that are new? Where does that collide with your faith experience?

2. How do you usually approach something? With an attitude of demolition or of renovation? Is that attitude the same when it comes to your faith?

3. What do your answers to the previous two questions tell you about yourself?

4. What would you say the story is that you currently live in? Where is it going? Is it coherent, or confusing?

5. There is a huge difference between convictions and opinions. What is the difference to you? Have you ever been hurt because someone confused the two? When it comes to faith in something you can't see, what are some of your convictions, and what are some of your opinions?

ABOUT THE AUTHOR

Jared Herd serves as the Creative Director for XP3, a division of the Rethink Group. For the past ten years he has traveled extensively, speaking to hundreds of thousands of high school and college students. During that time, he has served on staff at two churches on two different sides of the country—North Point Community Church in Alpharetta, Georgia, and as a teaching pastor at Rock Harbor Church in Costa Mesa, California, a church composed of thousands of college students. He and his wife, Rosanna, currently reside in Atlanta, Georgia.

Rumors of God
"Faith in God in action"
by Darren Whitehead
& Jon Tyson

From C.S. Lewis' classic work *Mere Christianity:* "This world is a great sculptor's shop and we are the statues. But there is a rumor going round the shop that some of us are some day going to come to life." In *Rumors of God*, Jon Tyson and Darren Whitehead share with readers how the rumors are true and will call Christians to a life that transcends the shallowness of our culture.

More Lost Than Found
"Finding God"
by Jared Herd

In *More Lost Than Found*, youth expert Jared Herd comes alongside anyone who has drifted from faith to reengage them with the truth they long to hear. In this refreshing, true-to-life message, readers find a companion for their faith journey, rediscover the truth they grew up believing, and are invigorated to lay hold of it once again.

With
"Connection with God"
by Skye Jethani

Instead of a life over, under, from, or even for God, what leads us into freedom and restoration is life *with* God. Written by Skye Jethani, managing editor of *Leadership Journal* and author of the award winning blog *Skyebox* (SkyeJethani.com), *With* identifies the need many Christians feel for a deeper experience of God in everyday life.

Close Enough to Hear God Breathe
"Intimacy with God"
by Greg Paul

Does the idea of intimacy with God seem far-fetched and irrelevant to your real, daily life? In Greg Paul's *Close Enough to Hear God Breathe*, readers discover a rich message recounting the story of a God who has been inviting all of humanity, and each individual, into His tender embrace since time began.

Available wherever books and ebooks are sold.